CREATIVE FLY TYING

CREATIVE FLY TYING

MIKE MERCER

Photography by Ted Fauceglia

Illustrations by Greg Pearson

WILD RIVER PRESS

Library of Congress Cataloging-in-Publication Data
　　Mercer, Mike.
　　Creative fly tying/Mike Mercer.—1st ed.
　　p. cm.
　　ISBN 09746427-3-8 (hardcover)
　　Fly tying. 2. Fly fishing. I. Title.

　　2004117106

Book and jacket design by Gregory Smith Design
Photographs of flies and materials by Ted Fauceglia
Fishing photos by the author and others as noted

Published by Wild River Press, Post Office Box 13360, Mill Creek, Washington 98082 USA

Wild River Press Web site address: www.wildriverpress.com

Printed in Thailand

10 9 8 7 6 5 4 3 2 1

DEDICATION

A FRIEND IS SOMEONE WHO TRULY WANTS THE BEST FOR YOU and gives whatever he can to make that happen. He looks for opportunities to spend time with you and relishes the memories you share. He stands by you in times fraught with pain, fear and despondency, celebrating good times with an open heart and a joyful laugh. A friend prods gently when necessary, showing you a better way.

I've been blessed with an embarrassment of good friends over the years—people who have given freely and honestly of themselves. Many have helped shape my values and beliefs. One, a relatively new friend, slipped in quietly under the radar of my comfort zone and changed my life forever.

Thank you, Willie, for giving generously of yourself in your most difficult of times; for showing me the right path; for laying out the tools for me to work with; for your uncompromising faith; for allowing me a glimpse of our Lord's sovereignty, a reflection of His glory and faithfulness in the heart and words of a common man. Thank you, Willie, my humble friend, for your incredible heart.

ACKNOWLEDGMENTS

I PENNED THIS BOOK, it's true, but without the help and inspiration of so many others, there would have been nothing to write. The list is far too long to be complete here, but there are some I simply must mention.

To Mom and Dad, who unwittingly launched me into a life and career in fly fishing, and who supported me totally and unswervingly, even in the early years when I'm sure they didn't really understand my obsession.

Kristi, my wife, and daughters Kalyn and Ariana, who support me with a minimum of eye-rolling.

Mike Michalak, my employer and friend for more than half my life.

Tom Pero, publisher, for believing in me and offering the luxury of free rein with this project.

Ted Fauceglia, for gracing these pages with his incomparable macro photography, and going above and beyond to make sure the tying sequences were *just* right.

Bruce, Dave, Jim and all my friends at Umpqua Feather Merchants for their faith and friendship over the years.

Kelly Galloup and Ted Leeson for their continuing support and encouragement during my inaugural voyage.

Greg Smith, graphic designer, for his magic in turning my simple words into a work of art.

John Dietz, Jim Murphy, John Foley and Craig Falk, with whom I've shared some of my most memorable days astream.

All my co-workers at The Fly Shop, who unflaggingly support my successes, and aren't afraid to let me know when I'm being ridiculous.

Ed and Donna Willett, faithful friends all these long years.

Denton Hill, my earliest mentor, for inspiring me to dream big.

Dave Stammet, who always seemed to make the time for a shy little kid who lived to fish—I miss you, Dave.

Rebecca, my sister, who had to clear the path of life before me, and who continues to inspire me today.

To my Father above, my strength and compass every day of my life.

CONTENTS

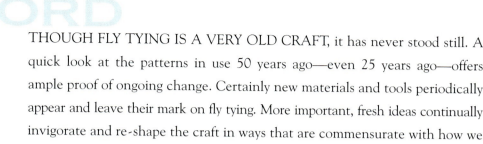

FOREWORD

THOUGH FLY TYING IS A VERY OLD CRAFT, it has never stood still. A quick look at the patterns in use 50 years ago—even 25 years ago—offers ample proof of ongoing change. Certainly new materials and tools periodically appear and leave their mark on fly tying. More important, fresh ideas continually invigorate and re-shape the craft in ways that are commensurate with how we think about trout streams and trout, and how we fish them. As a result, not only new patterns but whole approaches to tying evolve.

Some of the impulses behind this change come from outside fly tying itself and are, not surprising, more closely aligned with fishing. In the last half-century or so, I think two such forces in particular have pushed fly tying in new directions. The first is a widespread and systematized set of ideas about stream ecology, the life cycles of insects, and trout behavior, and a corollary emphasis on hatch matching. That artificial flies can be made to imitate bugs is hardly a new notion, but the conceptual dominance of this idea in trout fishing has never been stronger. The second force is one of sheer numbers—more anglers fishing fewer trout streams. The second of these has made the first an increasing necessity for successful fly fishing in many parts of the country. In a great many waters, trout have become more discriminating, better educated—and we are the ones who are teaching them. Fly patterns and the way we think about tying have changed because we have changed the fish.

There is another evolutionary impulse, however, that comes from within fly tying itself. I do not pretend to know how or why it occurs but it happens. In fact, it's happening now. Though pinpointing such things is difficult, I'd say between 15 and 20 years ago there began a tremendous infusion of new creative energy into fly tying. There were not simply more tiers, or more good ones— though both of these are true—but more ideas. The craft became increasingly improvisational as tiers experimented with new materials and techniques and, above all, new designs. The Adams ceased to be an automatic reference point for dressing dry flies and a Hare's Ear the benchmark in tying nymphs. Fly tying, of course, has always been marked by innovation; change is nothing new. But what has been striking in the past two decades are both the pace of change and the fertility of imagination that has played out in such a variety of directions. Nothing in particular suddenly blew the lid off more traditional tying, which, by the way, is flourishing as well. But alongside it is a newer creative momentum that, as I see it, is still accelerating and has produced some fascinating chain reactions as tiers first adopt, and then adapt, one another's designs. Not all the patterns coming out of this are destined for greatness; in fact, very few probably are. But the ideas themselves are undeniably interesting. If you tie flies, the sheer vitality in the craft these days is in and of itself quite a wonderful thing. I do not believe there has ever been a better time to be a fly tier.

Looking back at the recent developments in the craft, the impulses that shaped them and the directions they have taken, I think few tiers represent them as well as Mike Mercer. He didn't single-handedly initiate this "renaissance" in tying, and I'm certain he would never make that claim. In fact, one of its most remarkable features is that it's been a kind of leaderless, grassroots invigoration; new ideas have appeared spontaneously from a great many different places. By the same token, there's no question that Mike Mercer is among the tiers at the forefront of change. From their design rationale to the innovative uses and combinations of materials, his patterns embody some of the most interesting ideas that have emerged—and are still emerging—in contemporary fly design.

I have never met Mike Mercer. Like many tiers, I know him primarily through his patterns. I've tied them (in my own dubious fashion) and fished them with success, having learned of his flies from dozens of magazine articles and books that have appeared over the years—almost all of them written by other people. And like many tiers, I've hoped that Mike himself would one day sit down, pick out his top designs, and show how he ties them. Judged by that standpoint alone, *Creative Fly Tying* has been well worth the wait. The patterns are first rate; the text is clear and detailed; Ted Fauceglia's photography is typically flawless.

Despite their trim, sometimes elegant, detail, Mike's patterns aren't particularly difficult to tie. Some certainly require more steps than the average fly; but the steps tend to be routine procedures with which every tier is familiar. In fact, one of the hallmarks of his patterns is that, despite their appearance, they rely on relatively simple tying methods rather than elaborate techniques. You don't have to be a thread-handling magician or a wizard at spinning deer hair. But his designs are so tidily and seamlessly built that, while the materials and methods may be straightforward, reconstructing the tying steps from the finished fly is not always an obvious matter. The instructional sequences in this book will lead you through them.

But there's more to it than that. This is a different kind of fly-tying book. For starters, it's written by a fisherman, a *very good* fisherman. (I have it on redundant and irreproachable authority that the author is a vacuum cleaner on the water.) Take a look at his Reading The Water for instance. No other fly-tying text I have ever read argues, at the very outset, in the most conspicuous position in the book, that fly patterns run a distant second to presentation when it comes to catching fish. It happens to be true—but it's not the kind of thing professional fly designers urge in print very often.

It is not surprising then that the patterns themselves issue from a lifetime's experience fly fishing. For what you get here is more than merely a good tier showing you how it's done. This book lets you watch a fly designer's mind at work, from analyzing angling problems rooted in the appearance and behavior of aquatic food forms and the habits of fish, to translating those observations into finished architectures. It is a fascinating and enlightening process to follow, particularly when the designer is as talented—and as determined—as Mike Mercer.

Fully half of this book is devoted to accounts of how the fly patterns came to be, and certain parts of these stories are particularly intriguing, beginning with what might be called the "design logic" of a pattern. Nothing—at least nothing useful—is designed in a vacuum. There is a starting point and a rationale through which it takes the form it does. In designing a fly, say, a mayfly nymph, it seems reasonable to start with the insect itself, observing its size, shape, color, and so on, and working to replicate these in a fly pattern. Mike's starting point, however, is invariably the trout, asking the question, "What might the fish be seeing?" and looking at the insect through the eyes of the fish rather than those of the fisherman. This, as he readily admits, is an uncertain proposition at best. But what better choice do you have? He looks to discover what he calls the "meaningful features," the "visual highlights," the "triggers"—those particular characteristics of a food form that prompt a trout to bite. And those characteristics tend to be one of two kinds: the behavior of an organism, its mode of locomotion or mobility in the water; and its appearance with respect to light: translucence or opacity, glossiness or dullness, the way it reflects or scatters or transmits light, contrasts of bright and dark. These key features become the foundation of the design. Neither the theory of "triggers" nor the emphasis on the "optical properties" of a food form are original with Mike, but he is certainly one of contemporary fly tying's strongest proponents of these ideas. It is instructive to watch a pattern take shape according to these principles.

Perhaps the biggest gap in all design processes is the one between knowing what you want and knowing how to get there. So in *Creative Fly Tying* there is much talk of materials, weighing and assessing their relative merits, bringing to bear the kind of knowledge that only comes with long experience both tying flies and working in the fly-fishing business. And the information here—not just about materials, but about how one *thinks* about materials in relation to purposes—is both insightful and useful.

Discovering what works involves discovering what doesn't. And in the evolutions of these fly patterns, we see all the false starts, blind alleys, dead ends, miscalculations and mistakes that are inevitable—materials that failed to serve the purpose, flies that fell apart after one fish, ingenious architectures that finally proved just too damn difficult to tie. While such explanations might easily have been omitted in the interest of efficiency or ego, much would have been lost. Part of all invention is failure, and it is often the part that teaches us the most.

You may be surprised to see how often a couple of ideas come up in relation to Mike's designs. The first is "luck." There are really two kinds of luck in this book. One is the real thing, the genuine article, "lucky luck": the fortunate coincidence, the happy accident, the right-place-at-the-right-time kind of luck. And there's no question that the chance occurrence or serendipitous discovery is sometimes a component of success. As the saying goes, chance favors the prepared mind. The other, more common, kind of luck on display in this book is the kind you make yourself—through experimentation, adaptability, and persistence. It may in retrospect seem like stumbling across an answer, but it is hardly stumbling. It's working to solve problems.

The other and more elusive idea that crops up repeatedly in these design stories is "instinct," "gut reaction," "hunch"—that apparently sourceless sense that some idea about construction or materials will work. And part of this sense is undoubtedly traceable, through some now irrecoverable path, to a reservoir of personal experience; the actual connection has vanished, leaving only a gut feeling behind. But some of it, I think, is genuine instinct. You see it in anglers sometimes, that uncanny knack of knowing how, where, and when to find and catch fish. They can't really explain it; they just know. In designing patterns, Mike Mercer has "fly sense" the way some guys have "fish sense."

Whether it is gut feeling or luck, much about the process of invention is individual and idiosyncratic. Yet underwriting it all in this book is something that is shared by every good fly tier I've ever known. It is a kind of mental contradiction. On the one hand is an unquestioned faith that, for any given fishing situation, there is such a thing as a perfect pattern, a fly so intrinsically irresistible that it will ring the dinner bell every time. No one has invented it yet, and it may never be discovered, but it is out there somewhere in the ideal realm of the imagination. On the other hand is a distinct, clear-minded, rational recognition that the perfect pattern does not and could never exist. It is an impossibility. What fuels Mike Mercer's innovations in these pages—and indeed, what I think has fueled fly tying from its very beginnings—is this search for a perfect fly even while knowing it can never be found. It is completely illogical to hold these two ideas in mind simultaneously. But then perhaps that is how creativity is born.

Whatever its origins, you will find an abundance of creative ideas in this book—a long-awaited first from one of North America's foremost tiers.

TED LEESON
CORVALLIS, OREGON
January 2005

INTRODUCTION

SOME OF MY EARLIEST MEMORIES are of summertime camping with my family on the banks of a cascading mountain stream—accented by towering, scented pines; tame deer; and marshmallows blackened in a campfire beneath star-studded night skies. I was only five, but for weeks at a time I would rise with the sun, grab my little closed-face spin-casting outfit and precious green-lidded jar of salmon eggs, and make the trek past neighboring campsites, through the woods, to "the place where the fish lived."

Even at that tender age, I was absolutely enthralled with water and those things that resided within. Some days I fished without success, an outcome that conjured not disappointment but rather opened another door of fascination. On these occasions, I'd reach beneath large underwater stones and flip them, observing with a mixture of fear and enchantment the crawling aquatic denizens, some as long and as wide as my thumb. Searching for what seemed hours, my thrill knew no bounds when I'd finally discover my ultimate prey— a leather-skinned, fire-bellied salamander indigenous to this place. These magical creatures were the source of endless intrigue, both for their exotic appearance and gaudy color, and for the connection I felt for the watery wilderness in which they lived.

On other days I actually caught fish. I can still remember the drill: threading two fishy-smelling, lipstick-pink eggs onto a tiny gold hook, then lobbing them out into the clear, swirling depths. I would wait for that electrifying tap, that brief interface between me and another universe. When it came, I'd haul back on my rod and…and, well, I don't remember exactly what would happen next, but to listen to my mom tell it, she'd hear a bunch of excited yelling, followed by the sight of me, rod draped over my shoulder and bucking wildly as I dragged the hapless trout along the dusty path back to our tent. The Great Provider.

It's funny how different events impress themselves indelibly on children. That summer on upper Hat Creek set the template for the rest of my life. For me, the low rumblings of the early-morning Fish and Game trout-planting truck was an event that eclipsed even that of the ice-cream lady back home (though both created similar circus-like atmospheres, rank with the jostling and positioning of eager patrons). My lifelong passion for trout, water and all the creatures in the coldwater universe was ignited.

The smallmouth bass that changed my life: my first fish on a fly.

Following that summer vacation, I lived the insular, bucolic life of a young boy raised on a farm, outside Durham, California. I'd still rise early. Without a care in the world, I pedaled my banana-seated Stingray bicycle beneath snowing canopies of blooming almond trees, past endless acres of row-crops. Finally I'd arrive at the nearest streams—actually ingeniously contrived backhoe travesties, necessary water-carrying scars through an otherwise unblemished agricultural landscape. Scenic they were not, but for a naïve, budding angler, they were just fine. These ditches were filled with clean, fresh water. To me, they were unbelievably beautiful flows so many miles from any natural river or stream: water simply pumped to the surface via manmade pumps and wells, liquid still frigid from its subterranean coursings.

By all rights, these canals should have been absolutely sterile—they came out of a pipe, for crying out loud—but Nature, as she often does, had a pleasant surprise for me. Far from being lifeless dirt troughs, these artificial creeks had colorful small stones lining their beds and occasional weedbeds caressing their flanks. Most amazingly, there were fish.

Squawfish, I now realize. Back then they were the stuff of fishing dreams. How they made their way there through a maze of dams, screens and other well-devised impediments, I'll never know. But there they were. Try as I might, I never did catch one. The wonder of aquatic living creatures stayed with me, though, and my lessons of frustration and observation would soon serve me well.

About the time the Vietnam War was coming to a head, my family moved to a slightly less rural area on the outskirts of Chico. Our new house was still surrounded by orchards, but now we had neighbors and more paved roads. And down the street there was a real stream! I spent nearly every summer day there with Craig Falk, my new best friend and fellow fishing lunatic. The creek was small but it had character. Gentle riffles fed deep, sun-dappled pools, all cloaked in sycamore and blackberry bushes. It was loaded with fish. The best thing was, it was all ours.

Craig and I became expert worm anglers. We used our state-of-the-art Fenwick fiberglass rods and Garcia spinning reels to hook smallmouth bass, catfish, squawfish, suckers, an occasional trout, and a mysterious perch-like creature known to this day as "those flounder fish." Though we gradually branched out to local warmwater sloughs and mid-elevation trout streams (whenever our parents were gracious enough to provide transportation), it was the small neighborhood creek that taught us streamcraft and the nuances of reading water. It was into this diminutive flow that I first cast a fly and watched in wide-eyed disbelief as a guileless little bass glided under and inhaled it. My life changed.

John Andrews was fresh from the conflict overseas and attending Chico State University when he volunteered as a YMCA instructor. He worked with kids developing their skills in soccer, baseball and flag football. He was also passionate about fly fishing. John often brought groups of us on day trips to nearby streams, over to his place to see his treasure trove of fly gear, and to meetings of the local fly-fishing club. Once he brought my friend Steve Bruhn and me on a club outing to fish the Trinity River, where I caught one of my first-ever trout on a fly, a 13-inch rainbow that looked closer to five pounds as I was trying to get it in. More than anyone other than my parents, John was responsible for that first fly-caught bass on Big Chico Creek, and for that I will always be indebted to him. Though he long ago followed his career to Idaho, I remain in touch with him and am happy to report that he is still plying the streams and lakes there, much to the dismay of the fish.

About this same time, another pivotal event in my fly-tying and fishing career occurred: I bought a copy of *Selective Trout* by Doug Swisher and Carl Richards. I was absolutely captivated by this benchmark title, with its remarkable close-up photographs of aquatic insects and concise explanations of innovative tying and fishing techniques. During the next two years I must have read and re-read it a dozen times. A lifelong fascination with the bugs trout eat and how trout view them—and how this relates to tying effective imitations—was now forever etched into my psyche.

As I approached my mid-teens, I was fortunate to make the acquaintance of several individuals who nurtured my love of the sport. Dave Stammet and Mike Otkins, who owned Journey's End Tackle and Guide, a general fishing emporium in town, grew tired of my loitering around their shop and put me to work. I scooped minnows and counted nightcrawlers. I also learned the craft of building fly rods, the basic mechanics of the double haul, and how to make a few extra dollars on the side tying shad flies. On top of this, Dave took me on a few free guided fishing trips—fantastic adventures to me at the time.

With Craig Falk, my inseparable compadré, holding a morning's bounty from Big Chico Creek.

Just down the street, Walton Powell was busy creating his formidable legacy in cane, at a shop where his wife Earlene also tied flies commercially. Earlene was a superb fly tier and a most kind-hearted human being. Instead of throwing me out of their shop for vagrancy, she saw something in my inquisitiveness and taught me the finer points of constructing the Clyde Fly, Bivisible, Orange Palmer and many other traditional dries.

Perhaps most amazing in my mind was the attention given me by Denton Hill, local angler extraordinaire. He was a pioneer in exploring many remote fishing spots (often aiding in the "initial ascents") that are now developed, world-class destinations. I met Denton through the local fly-fishing club. He encouraged my obsession at every opportunity, including sharing with me many of his innovative tying techniques and ideas. On those occasions when Denton invited me over to his place, I was always awed by his collection of photographs and mounted trophy fish from around the globe. I loved the stories he told about them. He instilled in me the craving to travel and fish, to see the world with a fly rod. I continue having the honor of seeing Denton from time to time; the man is still a tremendous inspiration to me.

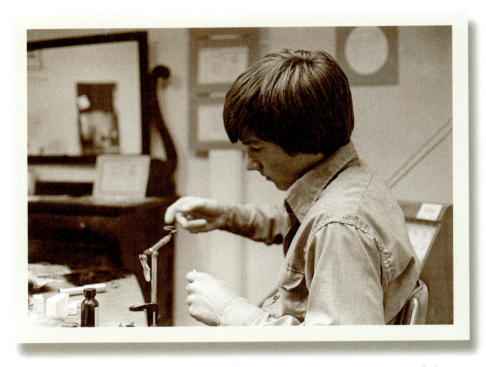

Seventeen years old, burning the midnight oil cranking out trout flies for a hungry market.

At this important juncture in my life, an amazing event transpired. It was an occurrence so fraught with life-altering ramifications that it almost overwhelmed me—I got a car.

Not just any car. It was a small pickup, given to me by my grandfather. It was the perfect vehicle to load up with a sleeping bag, ice chest, and every stick and stitch of fly-fishing equipment I owned, and head off to various wildernesses for adventures unknown. Looking back, now with children of my own, I can only imagine the worry I must have caused my parents: taking off on those extended forays, sometimes out of communication for days at a time.

Yes, I'm old enough to have one of these pictures haunting my past. John Andrews, my earliest fly-fishing mentor, and yours truly with evidence of a weekend's massacre on the Trinity River.

I subsidized my traipsing by opening a small fly-fishing store in the basement of my parents' home (Mike Mercer's Rod and Fly—I still have the sign!). The venture played host to countless all-night rod-building and fly-tying sessions. My parents earned what was to become their inevitable sainthood during the two years my shop existed. They financed my many expenses and helped me realize how much more was involved in a business of this sort than merely wanting to go fishing. I learned much. And I actually had a pretty cool little shop. It allowed me to meet a bunch of very nice people who stopped by during my limited open hours (you had to phone before coming over, to make sure I'd be there) to browse my modest selection of rods, flies and magazines.

One day, en route to a weekend of carefree, glorious hatch-matching on Hat Creek, I stopped off in Redding to check out a small shop I'd heard had just opened. It was called The Fly Shop. Mike Michalak introduced himself as one of the owners. We spoke for a while and then Mike, as if suddenly remembering something, inquired, "Is that your truck in the parking lot?"

"Yep. That's my fishing rig," I replied.

"You want a job?" he asked.

Turned out he was preparing to set up a booth at The Fly Shop's first major sporting show, and he needed someone with a pickup to help haul all the stuff.

"Sure," I said. *(Are you kidding—turn down a week's work with pay for an honest-to-God fly shop?)* That was more than 25 years ago. I've never worked anywhere else.

In the early days with the shop, I made my living as a fishing guide. I showed people the ropes on northern California's finest waters: Hat Creek, Fall River, McCloud River, Pit River, Trinity River, the upper Sacramento. I observed more about how fish react to flies in those five years than I'll ever learn again. The thing about guiding is that you push yourself to do everything possible to get your clients into fish. The more tricks you figure out, the better equipped you are to facilitate their success.

The backroom of Mike Mercer's home Rod and Fly Shop in Chico— piecing together a custom rod.

I worked from May through November. On my days off—I fished. I put myself in more fishing situations under a wider variety of conditions than can be imagined. Every day, dawn to dark, I lived, breathed and watched my rivers, from springtime salmonflies to late-season *Baetis*. I commanded, coddled and cajoled my anglers. I told them where to stand, which fly to tie on, and—if they were interested—why. I paid attention to their mistakes and learned from their successes. I knew where the fish would be and how to catch them. I became a total fishing bum. I spent nights at the bar, commiserating with clients and fellow guides, or at my vise fleshing out ideas spawned from the day's experiences. I had the time of my life.

Eventually it became too much. But I was fortunate. At the moment I recognized impending burnout, the shop came calling. Mike and his partner had been building a small mail-order dynasty while I'd been astream. Now they wanted me to help them run it.

Picture this: You've just spent the last five years closely observing trout feed in the wild and how they behave when offered faux food. Your head is filled with a constantly changing stream of ideas about how to tie flies to get the reaction you want from them. Suddenly, you're in one of the finest fly shops in the country, with every conceivable tying material and tool at your disposal. Get the picture?

I went nuts.

I'm still going nuts, creating new flies that I'm convinced will work better than the last ones. Though my principal job now is selling international fly-fishing trips through the shop's travel department, I still ogle each new material as it comes through the door, still scour every new book and magazine for fresh ideas and gadgets. I'm a hopeless fly-fishing junkie with an incurable addiction to the vise. Just as in those summers of my youth, I'm fascinated with the mysteries of life beneath the water. These days, it's mostly fish and bugs I investigate. But I still get excited over the occasional salamander.

MIKE MERCER
REDDING, CALIFORNIA
January 2005

READING THE WATER

An American classic: an idyllic afternoon on Montana's DePuys Spring Creek. Where to begin?

I KNOW, I KNOW, I CAN HEAR IT NOW. What is this, a fly-tying book or a fishing book? The truth is, I believe the two are inextricably entwined. But before you roll your eyes and page ahead, don't worry—this will be my last tangential foray before diving into individual patterns. Rivers, or more specifically the particular types of water we fish, have played such a major role in how I design my flies that I believe they need to be examined. Reading water is possibly the most fundamental skill to fishing success, a skill that can be learned and constantly improved upon.

Okay, just for the record, how many of you out there think your choice of fly is more important to catching fish than your presentation of that fly? How many say the presentation is more important? For all of those who, like me, wish the former were true, now would be a good time to pinch yourself and wake up. If you, like me, find flies captivating, wondrous bits of magic on a hook, welcome to the Romantics' Club. Truth is, presentation will win this chicken-or-the-egg debate nine times out of 10.

A poorly chosen fly, presented well, will still catch a few fish. Conversely, the perfect fly for a situation, presented poorly, is much less likely to experience success.

If you want proof, go to a deep, boulder-studded stream where you know fish are foraging heavily on large stonefly nymphs, and tie on a tiny midge pupa. Put on split-shot and bounce it along the bottom, just as you would the stonefly. You won't hammer the fish, but you'll tag a few, because you're putting it in their faces. Then tie on the best stonefly nymph in your box, the one that looks just like the naturals, and swing it on a tight line, an inch below the surface. Guess what? The fish don't even see the fly, so they never have the chance to take it. The bottom line is, you have to first know how to deliver the goods.

What I believe this old debate misses entirely, however, is the even more important issue of reading water. I've seen it a million times: An angler, rigged up correctly, with all the right flies from a local shop, fishes through a stretch of water slowly and deliberately. His presentation is good. So are his flies. Yet he catches little. A second angler, with essentially the same skills, follows him through, covers the water much more quickly, and cleans up. The difference? The first fly fisher had all the right tools but didn't know where to use them, while the second was reading the water correctly, seeing where the fish were most likely to hold. Not only did this result in increased hook-ups, but it was more efficient, as no time was spent methodically covering fishless water.

"Prime holding water" is a highly comparative term, one that is determined by two factors—availability of food, and an environment of safety for the fish. For the most part the key is: Find the food and you've found the fish. Should you find a run that has both deep water (protection from predators) and a steady supply of food, you'll likely have a gold mine. Fish will give up the depth, however, if the drifting buffet is adequately prodigious—for this reason, it pays to stay attentive at all times, even on familiar water.

Case in point: Probing the deep jade runs and riffle drops of California's McCloud River one crisp autumn day, I was surprised by a lack of bigger fish. This time of year, the resident rainbows always feed aggressively, putting on the feed bag before the cold weather sets in. In addition, huge, lake-run browns have left Shasta Lake and are scattered everywhere, ascending to their natal spawning grounds. Wading to my thighs, I had fished all of my favorite slots, using nymphal imitations of the giant orange caddisflies that were helicoptering clumsily around me. All I caught were a bunch of small fish, though, and I was beginning to lose confidence.

Was my fly wrong? Was there someone just up around the bend, fishing all the water in front of me? *What was I missing?*

I decided to wade back to shore, have a snack and regroup. As I turned around and began to wade out, I perfunctorily flipped my nymph and leader into the shallows between the bank and me. Trying to pick them up again, I discovered I'd hung the bottom. Berating myself for this annoying lapse of diligence, I waded up to the

A wild Russian rainbow trout that fell for a Gold Bead Poxyback Green Drake Nymph fished behind a black leech pattern in a deep, heavy "bucket."

shallows where it was hung and commenced yanking the rod in different directions. The watery explosion was so violent and unexpected it actually frightened me—it was only sheer luck the "rock" didn't simply snap me off on its initial, ripping run.

As I landed the gorgeous rainbow minutes later, it occurred to me that this was my first large fish of the day. It had been holding, strangely enough, in bankside water barely deep enough to cover its spotted bulk. A coincidence? An hour later, weary from wading down the middle of the slippery streambed, casting to the banks, I knew otherwise. The shallows were loaded with big trout, apparently (though I didn't figure this part out until the next day) picking off the oversized caddisflies as they migrated there to emerge. A classic case of finding the fish by finding the food, despite a total lack of traditional

Jim Murphy plying the challenging, slow-moving currents of a western spring creek. Such water demands an angler's utmost concentration and stealth.

turbulent convolutions on the water's surface). Also, I usually avoid sterile, light-colored cobble stream beds, no matter how perfect the water appears. Where they exist, darker, vegetation-covered rock bottoms seem to attract more trout, presumably due to their increased capacity for holding food.

Another streamside feature I never pass up is the inside, soft "corners" found where riffles drop and begin to flatten. These innocuous, typically shallow little flat spots are widely overlooked due to their lack of depth or significant current speed. In fact, they provide actively feeding fish an effortless place to hold, and a non-stop conveyor belt of food in the form of bugs that spin off the adjacent faster water. If fish are up eating hatching insects or terrestrials, these corners are unbelievably reliable.

deeper holding water.

In case I'm worrying you a bit here, don't stress—most fish feeding in shallow, non-traditional water are much easier to identify, though the former does illustrate an important possible occurrence. Another, more common variation would be large trout moving to shallow water to inhale adult winged stoneflies as they drop from overhanging tree branches. In most freestone river circumstances, however, your success will ride largely on your ability to identify the "sweet" water: flows that are deeper than those around them, and those that have strong current flows broken up by submerged rocks and other underwater topography (identified by seams and

Part of recognizing prime holding water simply comes from experience. While the illustrations above are money in the bank, remember to constantly push these boundaries, always keeping in mind that outside circumstances can affect where trout lie. If you are nymphing appropriate water in a hard-hit tailwater without success, for example, consider the effect of other anglers. That perfect seam on the edge of a heavy run may have been hammered before you arrived, forcing fish to edge out into deeper and faster water than normal. I routinely hook fish in water so deep and heavy, most anglers wouldn't give it a second look. The fact is that many such runs are carpeted with current-cushioning boulders, providing perfect habitat and incredible fishing for those in the know.

Finally, let me give you a few little tricks to help your water-reading skills and make you a better angler.

1. Be just a little more aggressive and observant than the other guys. Most good fly fishers take a cursory look at a piece of water and do a great job covering the obvious stuff. This accounts for 75 percent of the fish being caught repeatedly—with 25 percent remaining relatively unscathed. That 25 percent represents a huge audience you can have all to yourself. Find these trout by studying the river for clues to less-apparent holding water: subtle streambed depressions, vague seams and slicks in what appear impossibly heavy flows, or that cutbank on the far side of conflicting currents that you know most anglers won't bother with. Time and again, I've doubled my catch rate by relentlessly kissing the

Avoid spooking large brown trout, which often lie in water barely deep enough to cover their backs.

A textbook freestone river featuring riffles, runs, pools, pockets and rapids—classic water-reading classroom.

bank with my dry fly, while others carelessly pound the water a foot or two out. If you're like me, the prospect of hooking a fish in a pocket you know others have missed is tremendously satisfying.

2. Make a ritual of sometimes fishing familiar water from the side opposite that which you normally fish. Most of us—including me—develop the habit of approaching known water in the same manner time after time. It's comfortable. We know from experience where to look to find fish. Problem is, in many cases we're overlooking that 25 percent of the trout population described above.

How is that? Try it, and you'll quickly understand. In many cases, a piece of water will look totally different when viewed from the opposite shore. You'll notice holding lies appear in new places. You'll discover improved drift lines not possible from the other bank. And you'll even detect trout rising in spots you never before thought to watch. This is a neat trick; usually it's very enlightening.

3. Dry-fly fishing is a rush. Whether a hatch is on or we're just covering water to coax unseen trout up from likely lairs, the excitement and anticipation of seeing a snout suddenly appear from nowhere to engulf our fly is palpable. Sometimes we'll work unsuccessfully to a fish rising in a challenging spot, finally putting it down with errant casting or dragging drifts. When this happens, don't simply rush frantically off to find the next set of lips; take a minute to understand what went wrong, and figure out what you could have done better. Pretend the fish is still rising. Work on your presentation until you master the intricacies of the situation and are confident that, given another chance, you would probably succeed. This will force you to slow down and pace yourself on each riser (you'll enjoy yourself more in the long run) and to learn from your mistakes. Then, faced with a similar situation later in the day—or any time in the future—you'll be much more likely to experience a favorable outcome.

4. My last tip has nothing to do with reading water, but may be one of the more important clues I can give you to becoming a consistently successful angler. Fish do not like flies with crud stuck to them. You'll almost never catch a trout with a fouled hook—even the slightest trace of moss is enough to doom you to fishlessness. Whenever you nymph a grassy stream, or fish a dry in a river with floating debris, get into the habit of checking your fly constantly, every second or third cast. A pain in the butt? You bet, but do it anyway and you'll soon be inspecting it on autopilot and catching a lot more fish. As a benefit, you'll eventually develop an acute sensitivity to the slightest drag in your drift. This will alert you instantly to the presence of unwanted passengers on your pattern, and won't hurt in the strike-detection department, either!

Becoming proficient at reading water takes time spent on the stream. You have to experiment, fishing not just the water you know from experience holds fish, but also those other great expanses that puzzle and intimidate you.

Wonderfully, there is no magic way to achieve instant gratification in this discipline. You usually learn in tiny bites, occasionally stumbling onto major enlightenments, until one day you realize unfamiliar water no longer baffles you. Your eyes and brain automatically register the slight nuances of hydraulics and streambed—you unerringly see where the fish will lie. No longer do you search out only those specific water types you understand—now you see nearly all water as holding promise. You fish with confidence and a delicious sense of anticipation.

CHAPTER 1

GOLD BEAD POXYBACK GREEN DRAKE NYMPH

"OH, YEAH, MERCER. HE'S THE GUY WHO USES EPOXY ON ALL HIS FLIES, RIGHT?"

Such, it seems, is my legacy in fly tying, for better or worse. Actually, I'm not complaining, as the notoriety gained from this simple technique has opened many wonderful doors for me. And while many credit me with inventing the method, it isn't true. As with so many tying procedures, the Poxyback style came to me from the genius of others; I merely adapted their ideas to best suit my needs.

Perhaps the best place to start is the beginning. For me, as an innovative tier, that occurred nearly two decades ago, on a brilliant, late-autumn afternoon. The days were short and cold. Trout season's imminent demise was whispering in my ear, urgent and melancholy. Joining me on the withered brown grass banks of an Oregon stream were Rich Henry and Andy Burk, two anglers of whom I'll always be in awe. Rich, a legendary fly-fishing pioneer and guide, had been generous enough to invite me to join him and Andy, already longtime friends, for a busman's holiday on this river—his river.

GOLD BEAD POXYBACK
GREEN DRAKE NYMPH

RECIPE

HOOK: TMC 2302, size 10 or 12

THREAD: Olive 8/0 UNI or equivalent

TAIL: Three ringneck pheasant tail fibers

RIB: Copper wire

ABDOMINAL CARAPACE: Dark golden-brown turkey tail feather

GILLS: Aftershaft feathers from back of an olive-dyed ringneck pheasant rump or equivalent

ABDOMEN: Mercer's Select Buggy Nymph Dubbing, Z-Wing color

WING CASE: Same as carapace

THORAX: Same as abdomen

LEGS: Golden-brown grouse feather or henback equivalent

EPOXY: Devcon 5 Minute Epoxy or equivalent

HEAD: Same as thorax

BEAD: Gold metal bead, size to suit

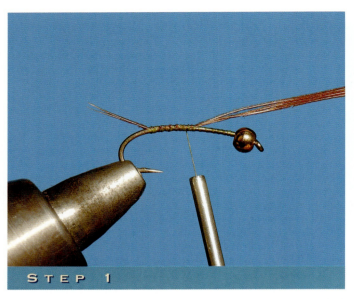

STEP 1

Slip the bead onto the hook, sliding it to a point right behind the hook eye. Create a sparse thread base, then select three fibers from the copperish-brown side of a ringneck pheasant tail feather, taken from the center of the entire tail splay. It's important to use these fibers, as the softer tan fibers found on the outside feathers typically won't separate and splay correctly. Use your fingers to make sure the fiber tips are aligned evenly, then pinch them to the top of the hook at a point just forward of the bend; tie them down. If there is thread in back of the feather tie-down spot, wrap the thread back over the fibers until you reach that original tie-down, while gently pulling the fibers back and upward. When you release the fibers, they should splay apart from each other slightly. If not, simply push them up from underneath with your thumbnail or the side of a scissor blade—this will accomplish the desired look. At this point, attach lead-free tying weight, if desired.

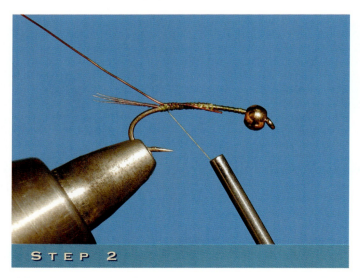

STEP 2

Attach the wire rib, tying it in on the upper, near side of the hook. Wrap the wire back over the shank to the point at which the tail was tied in. Clip off the excess about three quarters of the way up the hook shank, making sure you wrap the remaining wire solidly to the hook shank. This last detail helps ensure proper body proportions in the finished fly.

STEP 3

Tie in a slip of darkly mottled golden-brown turkey tail feather, securing it to the top of the hook shank. The tie-down area should mirror that of the wire rib, except for being on the top, not the side of the shank.

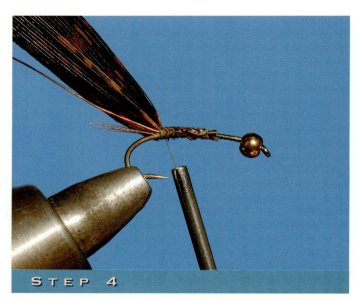

STEP 4

Repeat the above step with another slip of turkey tail.

STEP 5

Select and tie in an aftershaft feather from the back of an olive-dyed pheasant rump feather or equivalent. Attach it so that when it is pulled forward, it will lay flat, with fibers extending out to the sides of the fly. It's important to choose a feather that's not too long-fibered; when it is laid on top of the abdomen, the rearmost fibers should not lay back any farther than the tail feathers—a little shorter is preferable, for a realistic look in the water.

STEP 6

Repeat the above step, with another, matching aftershaft feather.

He'd navigated his old truck to a little-known stretch of the stream, on the way twisting through a maze of sorrowfully unkempt logging skid trails that effectively negated any need to swear Andy and me to secrecy. Just as I was preparing to delicately suggest to Rich that perhaps he'd missed a turn somewhere, he rolled the rig to a halt on a barren volcanic plateau, overlooking what appeared to be a dry, twisting ravine.

"Grab your rods," he called over his shoulder, disappearing down a barely discernible animal trail. I was dubious—there was no water in sight. In fact, it didn't seem possible that the sizable river we'd driven alongside only a few miles downstream could possibly flow through such an unimpressive gulch. When I voiced my uncertainty to Andy, he just grinned and vanished over the rim of the canyon. Feeling like Alice chasing the Rabbit, I plunged after.

The Gold Bead Poxyback Green Drake nymph is purposefully shaggy and designed for maximum underwater movement.

> ### "Grab your rods," he called over his shoulder, disappearing down a barely discernible animal trail. Feeling like Alice chasing the Rabbit, I plunged after.

A brief descent through thick underbrush and stunted pines delivered us, somewhat suddenly, to a small, magical pool. Seemingly all out of proportion to the trickling flows feeding it, the still water meandered for 30 yards before seeping away into the rocks. Arching an inquiring eyebrow silently to Andy, I was rewarded with another knowing smile, and a circled-thumb-and-forefinger "okay" sign.

We crouched soundlessly in the bushes at the water's edge, for long minutes heeding Rich's earlier warning about the absolute necessity for stealth. My eyes scanned the transparent water, searching at first for obvious movement, then for any sign of life at all. Nothing. It was like looking into a sterile aquarium. I stole a sidelong glance at Rich, who caught it and, slowly extending a pointing

STEP 7

Dub a slightly tapered abdomen, ending at about the same place the rib was tied off.

STEP 9

Bring both turkey tail slips forward individually, tying each down separately but directly on top of one another, at the same place as the aftershaft feather was secured. Note how this abdominal carapace forces the aftershaft gills to extend out to the sides.

STEP 8

Pull the aftershaft gills forward, and tie them down immediately in front of the dubbed abdomen.

STEP 10

Wind the wire rib forward evenly, being careful to avoid tying down the aftershaft gills, as much as possible. It can be helpful to separate the gills with a bodkin, making an opening through which to pass the wire on each revolution. Tie off the wire in front of the dubbed abdomen, and clip the excess.

Pull the doubled turkey slips back over the body of the fly at the same time. Wrap back over them to lock them into a rearward facing position.

finger, whispered, "See 'em?"

See what? I thought to myself. This pool is as dead as—and then, just as with those abstract 3-D picture books in the supermarket, my eyes locked into proper focus and I did see them. It was with a surge of disbelief that I realized exactly what I was seeing: huge, finning rainbows and brown trout carpeting the bottom of the pool, some in excess of the two-foot mark. The more I looked, the more I saw. Gaping, I nodded numbly back to Rich, who responded with one of his trademark chuckles. "Pretty nice fish, eh?"

A Poxyback Isonychia nymph that utilizes the same aftershaft feather gill technique as the Green Drake nymph.

> **It was with a surge of disbelief that I realized exactly what I was seeing: huge, finning rainbows and brown trout carpeting the bottom of the pool, some in excess of the two-foot mark.**

Form a twisted-loop dubbing "brush," and bring the thread up to a point just behind the bead.

Silently, Andy crept toward the top of the pool and Rich toward the tailout, leaving me with the prime, fish-choked middle section. For long minutes I was totally absorbed by the scene in front of me, watching with heart in throat as one monster fish after another glided up behind my nymphs, only to swerve off at the last moment. To no avail, I switched from pattern to pattern, until I remembered something Andy had mentioned to me earlier. "If all else fails today, go to a Hare's Ear with a dark wing case. I think the fish take 'em for a green drake nymph or something. Anyway, it's a good ace in the hole." Though never a big fan of the fly, I'd learned never to ignore a tip from Andy, so, dutifully, I took one from my box and knotted it on. Before I could even flick out a cast, I heard an enormous, belly-flopping splash, and looked upstream in time to watch a five-pound rainbow launch itself a second time, again shattering the pool's placid surface upon re-entry. As I watched him manipulate the big rainbow away from a sunken tree, I queried Andy on his fly choice.

Wrap the dubbing brush forward. Note how the twisted-loop technique gives you a heavy, bushy thorax—perfect to trim into the flattened, bulky profile desired for this imitation. Tie off immediately behind the bead and trim the excess.

STEP 15

Repeat the same process on just the top of the thorax. Don't trim the sides—you want some fibers to extend out here, to help create the illusion of a wide thorax.

STEP 14

Trim just the bottom of the dubbed thorax flat with your scissors, while leaving some bulk—you want a flattened thoracic profile, but not one that is wafer-thin.

STEP 16

Pull or snip off the rounded tip of your legs feather, leaving a V-notch. Lay the feather flat on top of the thorax, with the notch pointing toward the rear of the fly. The point of the V should be just short of the end of the thorax. Strip the fibers from the feather's stem at its butt end, so that there are barbs protruding to the sides of the hook beginning just behind the bead, where the feather is tied in. Clip off the remaining feather stem.

STEP 17

Pull the first wing case forward over the thorax, tying it down directly behind the bead. Don't stretch it too tightly, or the turkey strip will break into its individual fibers—this is not desirable, as it will allow the epoxy to seep through. Repeat with the second strip. Trim the excess.

STEP 18

Using a fine-tipped bodkin or needle, apply a coat of 5 Minute Epoxy to the wing case. Don't concern yourself with the thickness of the epoxy at this point—simply make sure you cover every bit of the feather. As soon as this is accomplished, and before the epoxy starts to harden, place another drop of the epoxy in the middle of the wing case; it will immediately self-level, giving you a beautiful, glossy effect. The size of this second drop will determine how thick or "high" the finished wing case will be.

"Hare's Ear," he called. "The one with a dark-turkey wing case!"

All right, you buggers, I've got you now, I gloated. *I've got the magic fly.* Turns out, it was Andy who had the magic, as did Rich—not me. After watching them both land numerous trout, I finally salvaged my pride with a pair of heavy-shouldered fish caught on a black leech, but I knew I'd taken the easy way out. They'd deceived their trout into eating nymphs; I'd just duped a couple of the most aggressive fish by eliciting a predatory, knee-jerk reaction. As we clambered back up to the truck, I asked Andy if I could see his nymph. At first glance, it looked identical to mine—same color dubbing, svelte abdomen, thorax spiky with picked-out guard hairs, dark wing case.

Uh-oh, I thought, *maybe it's not the*—and then I saw it. Though his fly had dried out in the cool afternoon breeze, the wing case seemed, strangely, to still be wet. To the touch, though, it felt dry, and a bit stiff. "Oh, that," Andy said nonchalantly. "That's a layer of head cement on the wing case. It's just a little something I like to do."

> **Though his fly had dried out in the cool afternoon breeze, the wing case seemed, strangely, to still be wet. To the touch, though, it felt dry, and a bit stiff.**

Well, I'll never know if that "little something" had anything to do with Andy's success that day, but it inspired and set in motion what would eventually become my Poxyback series. I knew I liked the look the head cement gave, but I wasn't quite sure why; it was just one of those inexplicable attractions.

Back home at my vise, I began experimenting, first with a fly I much preferred over the Hare's Ear, a Pheasant Tail nymph. Discovering that cement didn't do well when spread onto pheasant tail-fiber wing cases (it oozed off the uneven edges and seeped into the material itself), I substituted turkey tail. This worked much better, but as I admired my handiwork I experienced a nagging sensation (one with which I've become all too familiar over the ensuing years) that something was not quite right—that this was not yet a finished product. As I stared at it, I finally realized what it was: Although the cement covered the wing case, a lot of the fibers pushed up through it, creating a messy, uneven look. Solution? More coats of head cement, of course!

Problem was, when I layered on the three to four coats necessary to achieve the glossy look I preferred (letting each coat dry between applications), I had way too much time invested in each fly. I was a guide, for crying out loud—clients would routinely snap off 15 to 20 nymphs a day!

Working at a fly shop in between guide days does have its perks. Serendipitously, I happened to discover

STEP 19

As soon as the epoxy is fully hardened, dub a short collar between the wing case and bead.

STEP 20

The finished Gold Bead Poxyback Green Drake Nymph.

another tier who had beaten me to the punch. Hal Janssen, it seemed, had been tying stillwater nymphs with glossy wing cases for years, using a product known as Hard-As-Nails to achieve the shiny hump. Trying the product, though, I realized it wasn't going to be the answer for me. Like head cement, it tended to drip if applied too heavily, and usually required more than one coat to get a finished product. Also, Hal's beautiful bugs had wing cases that tended to match the body colors of the flies in question—for reasons I still hadn't yet grasped, I preferred the dark contrast that turkey tail gave.

Then I discovered Devcon 5 Minute Epoxy, and everything changed. Here was a viscous material that could be easily applied with a bodkin, and stayed wherever it was placed.

So, off to market I went, coming back from the local hardware store loaded with a cornucopia of super glues, clear caulking and epoxies. To make a long story short, caulking compounds weren't clear enough and were difficult to work with; super glues were too watery and wouldn't stay in place; and most epoxies took too long to set up, making the high-gloss, high-profile wing cases I desired problematic. Then I discovered Devcon 5 Minute Epoxy, and everything changed. Here was a viscous material that could be easily applied with a bodkin, and stayed wherever it was placed. No dripping, no soaking in. Best of all, I found that if I first used the bodkin to quickly cover every bit of the turkey, followed immediately with a fat dollop of epoxy placed in the middle of the wing case, it self-leveled, automatically giving a perfect high-gloss finish.

Interestingly, it was about this time that I figured out just why these wing cases were so appealing to me. I'd been seining *Ephemerella inermis* (pale morning dun) nymphs at a local creek, providing myself with preserved samples to tie from. When I dropped the first few into a glycerin-filled vial, I was immediately struck with their glistening ebony wing cases.

Wow, I thought, *these little guys are almost ready to pop.* Then it hit me. Their wing cases looked just like my epoxied turkey version! That's right—my original Poxybacks were created before I even realized what I was emulating. I probably shouldn't admit that, but I think it demonstrates the importance of keeping an open mind and an inquisitive eye toward new materials and techniques if you want to be an innovative tier. On countless occasions I've randomly discovered stunningly appealing procedures for which I had absolutely no use. When that occurs I'll catalog it, on paper if it's complicated or in my head if it's simple. There will come a time, I know, when the technique will be the final piece of a long-studied puzzle.

Nymphs of the mayfly _Drunella grandis_ or green drake are abundant in many of our western streams, and a much more important food source than I believe most people realize. They're a big mouthful, a veritable pot roast with legs, and are available to trout year round.

Which is, I suppose, a rather long-winded approach to explaining just one of the several triggering features built into this chapter's pattern, the Poxyback Green Drake Nymph. You see, once I understood the ramifications of the epoxied wing cases, I wasn't satisfied with simply adding them to existing patterns. I wanted to design a whole series of flies, using this as the common theme. For reasons you now understand, my first efforts went toward creating a PMD nymph. It was one of the first patterns I designed around a specific hook model, for correct anatomical effect, and to which I then added

other triggers, such as the Flashabou ribbing and marabou gills.

Nymphs of the mayfly _Drunella grandis_ or green drake are abundant in many of our western streams, and a much more important food source than I believe most people realize. Ever wonder why Hare's Ears work so well? How about Gold Bead Prince Nymphs, or Zug Bugs? A lot of these are greedily inhaled, mistaken for drake nymphs. And what's not to like? They're a big mouthful, a veritable pot roast with legs, and are available to trout year round. During their few short weeks of emergence they often migrate before hatching and can be wildly prolific. I've turned over rocks in Hat Creek and the McCloud River in late spring and observed seething masses of the chunky insects clambering clumsily about.

To provide the foundation for such a large, blocky insect, I settled on the Tiemco 2302, a mid-length hook with a strong wire and an understated yet graceful, lifelike curve. Because of the desirable increased shank length this hook gives me to work with, I often drop down a size from the larger, shorter-shanked hooks so often used for drake nymphs. I slide on a large gold bead, then, optionally, make eight to 10 wraps of a non-toxic, lead-substitute wire around the hook shank, pushing some (two to four wraps, typically) of the finished "coil" up inside the tapered hole of the bead. Though adding wrapped weight to my nymphs is not always the way to go, because I don't always like the way it makes flies behave in the water, with a green drake imitation it was the obvious call. Drake nymphs are poor swimmers. They tend to tumble awkwardly along the bottom if swept free of the streambed; adding additional weight will only help the presentation. If tying this pattern for a slower-moving spring creek, however, I'll omit the lead, and possibly even the bead.

Green drake nymphs have three fairly heavy tails. My first try at imitation was with lemon-barred wood-duck flank feathers; they're beautifully banded, just like the natural, but are a bit wispy, visually, and turned out to be trying until it looks and feels right.

Finally, the idea of using a ribbed aftershaft feather came to mind (not original—I remembered seeing it done in a book once). For those who don't know what this is, it's the small feather attached to the back of many birds' body plumage. As it turns out, the only ones in the correct color I could find at the time were ringneck pheasant rump models, so that's what I used. I now realize it was a lucky coincidence, as I've never again seen other birds' afterfeathers with the correct combination of plushness, size, and color. I suggest buying the packages of dyed-olive pheasant rump from a fly shop, then peeling the afterfeathers off the rump hackle, and preparing them by stripping off the messy stuff at the bottom of the stem.

Before tying in the aftershaft feather, though, remember the rest of the abdomen. When I was designing the fly, I decided on a dubbed abdomen, as I could taper a body to whatever dimensions I desired (easy.) Over the top of this, I would lay two afterfeathers flat, so the "gills" extended out both sides of the dubbing (two steps; not so bad). Then, to emulate the dark, armored appearance of the naturals' carapace, I felt doubled slips of turkey tail would be perfect (how many steps was this, again?). Finally, I chose a copper wire rib, to both segregate the aftershaft "fluff" into equal and separate gills, and to hold all this material in place.

Don't be afraid to recognize blind alleys, retreat, and explore new options. No one gets it right the first time, every time; settling for an okay result will doom you to mediocrity.

natural, but are a bit wispy, visually, and turned out to be too fragile for a big nymph. Next came golden pheasant tail fibers—they were the right size and nicely mottled, but unfortunately also proved frail. Finally I just went with ringneck pheasant tail fibers. Though not striped, they provided the correct profile and were very resilient; the fish don't seem to give a hoot about the mottling.

The abdomen design, I felt, was the key to creating a successful fly. Why? In a word, gills. Place a green drake nymph in an aquarium and let it stroll around. The first thing you'll notice, aside from its impressive bulk, are the oversized, constantly undulating gills. Unlike copying smaller natural nymphs, when I often simply tie in single clumps of marabou and call it good, the sheer size of the drake nymph makes it quite apparent that the gills are all individual, separately vibrating entities. I first decided to tie in a dozen tiny, separate little bunches of marabou, but somewhere between gills number four and five realized what a stupid idea that was, and regrouped. This is an important part of innovative tying, by the way. Don't be afraid to recognize blind alleys, retreat, and explore new options. No one gets it right the first time, every time; settling for an okay result will doom you to mediocrity. Keep

Seriously, it's really not a difficult procedure, and the finished product is phenomenal. The hardest part usually is getting the various materials tied on in the correct order. Just remember to tie them on in reverse sequence: ribbing wire first, followed by two slips of turkey tail, then the afterfeathers (I found that tying the feathers in by their tips, then folding them forward, works best), and finally the robust, slightly tapered, dubbed body. Then, when the dubbing is done, everything is in place to pull forward and tie down. One suggestion: When winding the wire rib forward, wiggle it back and forth slightly as you bring it through the afterfeather. This lessens the incidence of tied-down afterfeather "gills," and gives a nicer appearance to the finished fly.

Well, we already know what the wing case is going to be: a turkey-tail slip—eventually lacquered with 5 Minute Epoxy—right? So I won't belabor this, but I will add one tip: When tying larger Poxybacks, I like to tie in two identical slips, one on top of the other. That way, if the original feather splits apart when pulled forward over the thorax, the second acts as insurance, retaining the solid feather base necessary to spread epoxy on. If you tie a lot of these, it's probably a wasted step, but it doesn't take much extra effort. Also, due to the large thorax they will be covering, be sure to make the slips quite wide.

Green drake nymphs remind me of those Olympic-caliber weight lifters you see on television—enormous upper bodies perched on short, stout legs. To achieve this bulky, oversized thorax silhouette, I decided to use a twisted dubbing-loop technique. Many tools are sold to help with this—I prefer the Dyna-King model because of its hands-free spinning feature. After forming a large thread loop, put the twister tool into the bottom, and insert several sparse clumps of dubbing, forming a "tower" of dubbing inside the loop. Give the tool a whirl, and you'll end up with a heavy, ragged dubbing brush. Doesn't look like much, but don't worry—it'll be perfect. I like to remove the twister tool at this point and clip my hackle

perfection. If, however, you've ever tried to knot six small rubber bands, and then clip them to size, followed by the nearly impossible task of getting each one of them tied in correctly, you'll understand why this technique never made it past the prototype stage.

Instead, I opted for taking a dark, mottled hen-back feather and pinching off the tip. I then peeled off all of the fluff at the base of the feather's stem, and tied the remaining feather in, laying it flat on top of the thorax with the missing tip end pointing toward the rear of the fly. Now, when you pull both turkey-slip wing cases forward and tie them down just behind the bead, you have nice, heavy legs extending out each side. Finish by spreading on the epoxy, dub a small head and—*whew!*—it's done.

Green drake nymphs remind me of those Olympic-caliber weight lifters you see on television—enormous upper bodies perched on short, stout legs.

pliers on at the same place, to keep the loop from untwisting.

Using the pliers, slowly wrap the dubbing brush forward, each rotation tight to the last, forming a fat, hairy, ugly ball of a thorax, ending just short of the bead. Now, to make it pretty, take your scissors and trim it as flat as possible on the top of the shank, and only a little less flat on the bottom (you want to retain a little bulk on the bottom, as the actual bug is pretty beefy). How much you choose to trim the sides of the thorax dubbing is up to you, but as a general rule a slight amount of dubbing should extend out each side of the turkey wing cases when they're pulled forward.

Though not particularly effective as swimming appendages, a green drake's legs are quite large and pronounced, so are certainly worth addressing. My original legs were tied from small-diameter round rubber, with little knotted joints. To this day I believe they were absolute

If asked to pick my personal favorites among the patterns I've developed over the years, the Poxyback Green Drake Nymph would be close to the top of the list. It's certainly not the quickest tie, but neither is it the most involved. It was one of my first attempts at designing as many meaningful features into an insect-specific pattern as I could without careening off into the realm of absurdity. Best of all, the fly has longevity. It's become one of my most durable inventions, gradually becoming more known and appreciated every year since its conception. I know plenty of anglers who now count it among their most reliable prospecting nymphs, as well as a favorite at drake time. A bigger compliment I cannot imagine.

COPPER BEAD MICRO Z-WING CADDIS

THE FISH COUGHED, I SWEAR IT. Not a croak, or regurgitative belch—these could all be explained away as involuntary reactions. No, this prettily spotted, sow-bellied porker of a lower Sacramento River rainbow pushed a throat-clearing little bark out its larynx just as sure as you would hack a frog from your own throat. *Too weird.*

Half expecting a reproachful diatribe on my thoughtlessness to pop from its vigorously working jaws, I quickly slid the trout back into the clear flows, more than a little unnerved. Only then did I notice the squirming detritus on the back of my hand. I laughed out loud. The fish had coughed, all right, but only in response to my unwittingly applying the Heimlich maneuver to its grossly distended belly. Imagine locking an eight-year-old inside a candy store for a day, and you'll get the idea of my trout's predicament. I had merely provided temporary relief from its unstoppable gluttony.

COPPER BEAD Z-WING CADDIS

RECIPE

HOOK: TMC 2457, sizes 14-20

THREAD: Olive 8/0 UNI

RIB: Chartreuse 3/0 Monocord or equivalent

BODY CARAPACE: Dark golden-brown turkey tail feather

BODY: Mercer's Select Buggy Nymph Dubbing, Z-Wing color

WING PADS: Light dun to dark dun Z-Lon yarn, to preference

COLLAR: Mercer's Select Buggy Nymph Dubbing, caddis green color

HEAD: Peacock herl

BEAD: Small copper metal bead

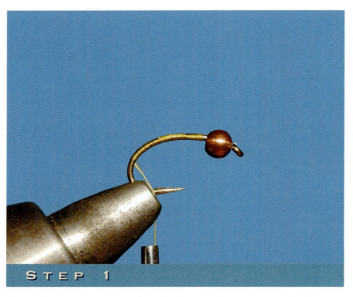

STEP 1

Slip the bead onto the hook, sliding it forward until it rests against the eye of the hook. Form a thread base that ends well down into the bend of the hook.

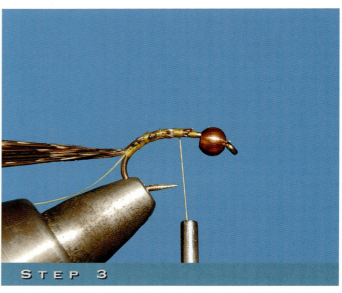

STEP 3

Wrap on a slip of darkly mottled golden-brown turkey tail, keeping it positioned on top of the hook shank.

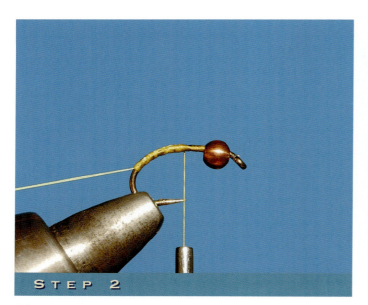

STEP 2

Tie in the thread rib.

STEP 4

Repeat the above step with a second turkey tail slip, tying it directly on top of the first.

Dub a length of thread using the simple twist-on method. Begin wrapping the dubbed body immediately forward of the turkey tail slip tie-ins.

Switch to an amber color to imitate a *Hydropsyche* caddisfly pupa, which is available to trout all season long.

It was no surprise to find that the fish's gift consisted of half a dozen caddisfly pupae, only slightly the worse for wear from their recent experience. The springtime *Rhyacophila* caddisfly emergence was in full bloom. What caught my attention was the insects' coloration. They had dark backs and bright-green bellies. I looked at the nymph dangling from my tippet—it was green, 360 degrees. The naturals had exquisitely bright-emerald inter-segmental banding of the abdomen; mine had none. The partially-emerged wings of the bugs were milky transparent; my pattern had no wings, and those of every fly in my box that did were dark and opaque. Finally, the heads of the tiny caddis were darkly iridescent. The head on mine…wasn't.

The fish had coughed, all right, but only in response to my unwittingly applying the Heimlich maneuver to its grossly distended belly.

The Lafontaine Deep Sparkle Pupa that hung from my leader that day many years ago was the hottest thing going. Based on countless hours of underwater observation, it was perhaps the first fly to specifically incorporate features emulating the distinct flash from trapped air on an emerging caddis pupa's body. I knew then as surely as I do now that I would never be the creative genius that Gary Lafontaine was—his flies were remarkable not just in their ingenuity, but also in the way they caught fish. That they remain just as productive to this day is, I believe, the true measure of his innovation. Nonetheless, as I observed the obvious differences between the fly and the naturals, I couldn't help wondering: *What if?*

In my experience, we fly fishers typically don't know nearly as much as we think we do. I vividly recall a sunny June afternoon many summers past, wading thigh-deep in the rollicking currents of lower Hat Creek, putting on a clinic for a local fly-fishing club. A warm breeze buffeted

The finished dubbed body, covering about three-quarters of the available hook shank—note that it is a relatively heavy abdomen and only slightly tapered.

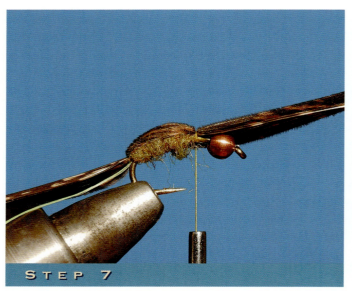

Pull the first turkey tail slip forward, tying it down in front of the dubbed body. The turkey should not extend more than halfway down either side of the dubbed body. Do not pull the turkey too tightly forward, as this will cause it to split into segments. This is not desirable, as it allows the underbody to poke up through it.

Bring the rib forward. The last two wraps should be spaced slightly farther apart than the first few, creating a realistic-appearing segmentation. Tie off the rib, and trim both it and the excess turkey slips.

Repeat the above step, laying the second turkey slip directly on top of the first.

Loop a piece of Z-Lon yarn, and tie down the vertex of the loop to the hook shank, immediately in front of the fly's body. Each end of the yarn should be sticking out to opposite sides of the fly.

STEP 11

Trim these yarn wing cases to about three-quarters the length of the fly's body.

STEP 12

Dub a bright collar, taking up about half the remaining hook shank. This collar should be slightly larger in diameter than the adjacent body.

clumsy salmonfly adults to the water's surface, and I was demonstrating to a rapt audience the importance of a good dead-drift presentation.

"All right," I shouted above the noise of the water gurgling against my waders. "First, cast your dry fly above and beyond your intended target." *Oohs* and *aahs* emanated from the crowd as I punched a size 4 Wounded Mallard 70 feet, skipping it beneath low-lying tree branches on the far bank.

"Then, lift your rod to skate the fly into position, simultaneously snapping an upstream mend into the entire floating-line section of the presentation." There came murmurings of admiration as the mended line fell perfectly into place above the fly.

Head-on view—note all the color contrasts built into the design, and the defined abdominal segmentation.

A warm breeze buffeted clumsy salmonfly adults to the water's surface, and I was demonstrating to a rapt audience the importance of a good dead-drift presentation.

"Now, drop your rod tip and begin to feed line out. You'll want to impart a slight twitching to the drifting dry—remember that trout are used to seeing these floating sirloins struggling feebly on the surface. Finally, at the end of the drift you'll want to strip your line in quickly and move on to your next cast. Fish don't see salmonfly adults under the water, so swinging it like a giant wet fly is just a waste of time." Here I observed—a bit smugly—that people were frantically scribbling notes.

WHAM! No sooner had my fly pulled beneath the water at the end of its drift than a rod-jerking yank and corresponding surface boil telegraphed an unmistakable grab to my now somewhat puzzled audience.

"Yes, well...occasionally *little* fish will grab it on the

STEP 13

Tie in two to three peacock herls by their tips, in front of the collar.

STEP 15

Holding both the thread and the twisted herls, wrap a "head" out of the peacock.

STEP 14

Twist the herls around the tying thread three to four times, to improve the peacock's durability.

STEP 16

The finished Copper Bead Micro Z-Wing Caddis.

swing." I began lamely to backpedal: "You know, young and aggressive, having to compete for food with the bigger trout." I saw pencils flipping over as people begin to erase things in their notebooks.

"Yeah," I continued, "this guy's just a little dinker— just a fluke" when WHAP! My "little fish" turned its

drowned salmonfly adults beneath the water's surface. My point? As fly fishers and tiers, we only know what we know. To push those limits, to get beyond the mentality of always tying on a Gold Bead Prince Nymph because it usually works, is what I really enjoy, and what keeps the sport interesting and challenging.

To push those limits, to get beyond the mentality of always tying on a Gold Bead Prince Nymph because it usually works, is what I really enjoy, and what keeps the sport interesting and challenging.

head and bored deep, stripping all the slack line from my fingers and coming tight to the reel. I watched in dismay as the (now obviously respectable) fish leapt dramatically, starting a good-natured barrage of derisive comments from my shore-bound spectators, and flushing my credibility down the toilet.

What had gone wrong? Nothing, really. This incident was just a slightly more-painful-than-usual example of the constant process of discovery that goes on as we fish. I thought I knew the rules of the relationship between trout and stoneflies, but I really only knew part of the story. As I observed more closely over the next few days—and as I experimented with varying patterns and presentations—I came to realize that fish often do see

Back to the coughing trout. So there I was, fishing a little caddisfly nymph that worked great, but which, at least in my hand, looked very little like the actual insect it was supposed to be imitating. Most exciting to me, the real bugs looked different than any caddis pupa pattern I'd ever seen. The thought of designing a completely unique imitation from scratch, using the visual highlights I observed, enthralled me.

Watching a tiny pupa wriggle around in a puddle of water trapped in my cupped hand, seeing how it often affected a "hunched" profile, I immediately decided upon the hook I would use. Tiemco hooks had just come onto the market. While they were considered very expensive at the time, their chemical sharpening made them so clearly superior to any other hooks that we all just gritted our teeth and paid the price. One newly introduced model was considered bizarre, and had been widely spurned by many tiers: a super-short-shanked, huge-gaped hook that went by the model number 2487. My trend-setting friend Andy Burk was literally the only person I knew bucking the resistance, utilizing it to create his groundbreaking Hunchback series of mayfly nymphs. It was also perfect for this job, I was certain.

Remember, this was a long time ago, before a lot of modern tying materials became available. Many synthetics (even the metal bead heads so common today) were still years from coming on the scene. So when I pondered the best choice for a dark abdominal carapace, I thought not

I had purposely chosen a vivid green thread to rib my pattern, based on the visually electric inter-segmental banding of the naturals. During the years since, I've experimented with other materials (a thread rib is *so boring*), but interestingly, I keep returning to the original. Flashabou, Krystal Flash, colored wires—none are more functional or give a better look, in my opinion, than this brightly-colored string. As I wound it forward through the abdomen, I also discovered another, totally unplanned, advantage of the doubled turkey carapace: When snugged down into the thickened turkey bed, the thread produced symmetrical indentations that perfectly imitated the natural's body segments. Thus my motto: Better lucky than good.

> I suspected then, as I still do today, that fish often respond more specifically to the contrast of varying colors on a fly than they do to the colors themselves. It would seem that attempting to exactly duplicate an insect's color as it appears to our eye may be a futile endeavor.

of Thin Skin, Scud Back or Medallion, but of the limited natural feather choices available at the time.

I finally settled on dark golden-brown turkey tail, as it was soft, easy to work with, and readily available. A fortuitous choice, I still believe, as it incorporates an irregular mottling and microscopic "hairiness" not normally associated with synthetics, but very lifelike. I started the fly by tying in a length of bright-green thread, which would act as a rib, followed by two slips of the turkey, one on top of the other. This way, if the bottom strip split when pulled over the abdomen, showing dubbing color through the breach, the second strip would cover the imperfection. Following Andy's lead, I wrapped them into place halfway back through the hook's bend—this would employ the hook's shape to give the desired curved-body silhouette.

I suspected then, as I still do today, that fish often respond more specifically to the contrast of varying colors on a fly than they do to the colors themselves. It's also been shown that fish see colors differently than humans do. Considering the lack of homogenous color schemes in many of Nature's creatures, it would seem that attempting to exactly duplicate an insect's color as it appears to our eye may be a futile endeavor.

Perhaps more important is to emphasize the natural contrasts that occur on an insect's skin, using a variegated dubbing to better emulate the mélange of hues most bugs exhibit. As an added bonus, this style of mixed color dubbing may also increase the chances of showing a fish the one "right" color that may provoke a feeding trigger. So I mixed up a dubbing utilizing five separate colors, with an overriding caddis-olive theme. With this tied in as an abdomen, with the turkey pulled over the top, I felt I had achieved my color and contrast goals.

As I mentioned previously, the semi-formed wings of the pupae I used as the original models for the Z-Wing Caddis had a milky transparency that resisted precise description; not quite clear or even light-colored, exactly, but definitely not the dark shade so often seen on caddis emergers. Not realizing that the wings generally darken as the emergence progresses, I was sure I'd made a historic discovery, and excitedly used a light shade of then-new Z-Lon yarn fibers as imitation. So sure was I that this single feature would revolutionize the way pupae would be tied in the future, I named the fly after the yarn used for the step.

In retrospect, it's almost a shame the fly worked so well right out of the chute, as it only served to feed my uneducated delusions. In fact, though you rarely see it offered as such, I've found substituting dark gray or even black Z-Lon fibers for the wings on this pattern produces a fly that often works just as well. I still like to think that the pale colored wings were a nice touch, though.

Many people have asked me why I added the middle collar of brilliant chartreuse to this fly. My answer is always the same: good question.

"Does it imitate some overlooked idiosyncrasy of caddis pupation?"

Not that I'm aware of.

"Inspired by the style of some great tying mentor in your past?"

Beats me.

Sometimes, when I'm experimenting, strange impulses spring unbidden into my mind. Most often, these unusual notions seem not to make much sense, but I've learned to not disregard them completely. Such was the case with this band of color—something told me the contrast would result in a pattern fish would find more attractive. Not very scientific, is it? I suppose if we knew all the

**What do two of the greatest nymphs of all time—the Pheasant Tail and Gold Bead Prince—have in common? Peacock herl.
What would I choose, with a gun to my head, as the single greatest tying material available on the planet?
Next question.**

answers, this would be a pretty boring sport. Certainly, the fly catches fish with or without it, but as long as I'm at the tying bench, it stays.

What do two of the greatest nymphs of all time—the Pheasant Tail and Gold Bead Prince—have in common? Peacock herl. What material glitters with a multi-hued iridescence that perfectly mimics nature, because it is, after all, from nature? Peacock herl. What would I choose, with a gun to my head, as the single greatest tying material available on the planet? Peacock herl. What did I choose for the forward collar on this pattern? Next question.

It's an interesting footnote that while this particular color of Z-Wing Caddis was the first of its kind, until the advent and popularization of metal beads its popularity was in serious doubt. Much more well-received initially was its dapper olive progeny, and eventually the amber offspring as well. And in fact, the gold-bead version of the olive quickly became the popular favorite, leaving the caddis green in the dust. It wasn't until I started experimenting with copper beads that this little fly found its niche, and in fact has now been embraced as the most widely accepted and used variation.

Five thousand coughing trout can't be wrong.

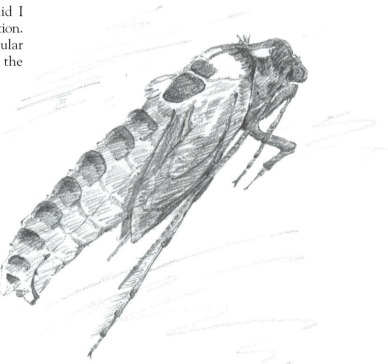

PROFILE SPINNER

I DROPPED THE ANCHOR SILENTLY, letting the coiled nylon rope slip smoothly through my fingers. The leaden mushroom dragged briefly across the marl bottom, sending up small explosions of suspended silt before catching. My johnboat swung neatly to a gentle stop 60 feet above a pod of rising trout. Perfect.

Fall River was its normal, classic self. Standing on the seat of the pram, I looked downstream and observed the fish as they tipped up rhythmically in the gentle, air-clear currents, methodically intercepting tiny floating snacks. I could see their spotted snouts pausing momentarily in the air, suspended strangely as they vacuumed the water's surface like fat carp. This was the upper river in early June, and there was no question what they were feeding on: Northern California's Fall River hosts one of the most concentrated and dependable early-season pale morning dun (*Ephemerella inermis*) spinner falls of any spring creek on the planet. Each morning on a half-mile stretch of meandering flows bordered by meadow grass, wildflowers and nesting cinnamon teal, millions of perfect little mayflies finish their ephemeral lives by giving birth to a new generation.

PALE MORNING DUN

RECIPE

HOOK: TMC 100, sizes 14-18

THREAD: Camel UNI 8/0

TAIL: Blue-dun spade-hackle fibers

ABDOMEN: Rusty turkey biot

WING POST: Macramé yarn, combed out

THORAX: Rusty brown Superfine dubbing

DOWN WINGS:
Dun Z-Lon yarn fibers

PARACHUTE HACKLE:
Blue-dun dry-fly hackle

STEP 1

STEP 2

Pull a sparse clump of fibers from the side of a spade feather from a good dry-fly neck. If you've never used these feathers before, there are a few of them located at the "outside corners" of every high-quality rooster neck, right where the small (size 14-16) and larger (10-12) hackles meet. You can recognize them by their wide profile and unusually long, stiff fibers, which are noticeably unlike the long, narrow silhouette and short fibers of the other dry-fly neck hackles. The sheen, translucency and flexibility of these fibers make what I believe to be perfect spinner tails. Making sure the fiber tips are aligned, tie them to the top of the hook; I prefer a single straight bunch coming off level with the hook shank, or with just a slight splay. Though I rarely choose to split the tail on this pattern, it's fine to do so for the sake of realism—just be sure to keep the fibers fairly short, approximately the length of the body, the same as with a single tail. This will keep the fish's snout from accidentally pushing away the fly when it rises, a potential problem with extra-long tails.

Trim a single biot from the feather stem. If you look at the cut section of the biot from the perspective of the trimmed end, you'll see the feather has a concave configuration running down its entire length. To achieve the desired "ridged-edge" segmented effect, you need to tie in the pointed end of the biot about mid-shank. Wrapping back over it, make sure that both edges of the biot curve away from you. Imagine the biot is a drinking straw that's been cut in half lengthwise—you tie it in so the imaginary cut edges face away from you, with the rounded side toward you. Wrap back over the biot to the spot where you tied in the tail, then back forward.

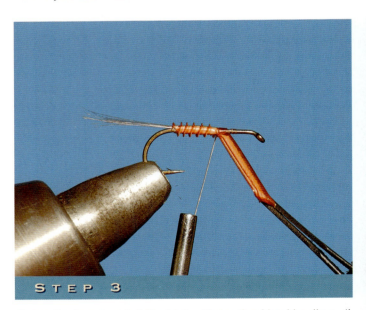

STEP 3

Using a pale-olive color scheme allows the angler to cover a wide array of smaller mayfly species.

Grasp the loose end of the biot with a pair of hackle pliers. (I recommend the J. Dorin brand pliers or equivalent: They grip the biot securely without slipping or cutting the feather and have small, maneuverable tips.) I find that a thin layer of Flexament applied to the hook shank before the biot is wrapped improves the fly's durability. Wind the biot forward with evenly spaced wraps, tying it off at approximately the mid-point of the hook shank.

STEP 4

Comb out a length of braided macramé yarn, slightly longer than you want the wing post to be high. It's easier to trim it to the desired length later than try and guess the correct dimension at this point. I like to use a mix of colors. My choice is based primarily on what's easiest for me to see under various glare conditions on the water. Normally I'll have one color facing forward and the other back. Begin tying the yarn to the top of the hook about a quarter of the way back from the eye, wrapping back toward where the biot was tied off.

STEP 5

Before you actually reach the biot tie-down, clip the yarn even with that spot, and then continue winding back until you've securely wrapped down all the butt ends of the fibers. Wind the thread back forward, and create a bump immediately in front of the wing post, effectively forcing it to stand upright.

It's an incredible thing to witness: incomprehensible numbers of tiny, pirouetting insects, each nearly transparent individually, but so dense in total as to blur the vision, making landscapes beyond seem to waver slightly. Then, eggs dropped, the spent mayflies fall to the water. As I watched, floating mats of the dying creatures drifted by, and into the suctioning maws of trout below. I briefly considered how foolish it was even to attempt to lure a trout with my fly, with so many hapless naturals to choose from. Get serious, I told myself. As if with 30 big trout gulping within casting range, I might just sit and watch!

Experience told me the best mornings for fishing were those that produced the lightest numbers of mayflies; unfortunately, this was markedly not one of those occasions. On the plus side, I also knew from previous encounters that these fish were very catchable. They took up feeding positions mere inches below the surface, allowing gluttonous feeding with a minimum of effort— this made their visual windows quite narrow. So intent were the trout on gorging themselves, they took scant notice of flies and leaders dragged continuously near their field of view. Even if I managed to spook them, it took less than a minute for their hoggishness to kick in and bring them back up.

Profile Spent Caddis, designed to float high and be seen easily, yet with the entire body beneath the surface film. This is a terrific pattern for broken water.

On the downside, the pattern had to be quite accurate to get a grab, and accurate meant fishing a fly that looked exactly like the other 3 million insects drifting down alongside it. On the upside…well, it was a beautiful morning, and this beat the heck out of working!

As with any heavy spinner fall, I knew to pick out a single fish and work to it exclusively, resisting the urge to simply feed my fly down into the melee of lips, which would result in a lot of fruitless presentations. The extremely narrow feeding lanes demanded surgically accurate drifts. To be even four inches out of the fish's feeding window was unacceptable—the fish simply would not move that far. They didn't have to.

Another trick was to time a particular fish's rhythm.

STEP 6

Wrap a thread base up the bottom of the yarn post, just as you would for any parachute. Make it substantial—better a little too long than too short.

STEP 8

Dub a sparse thorax, beginning by covering the yarn post tie-down, coming forward and locking the spent wings into place, and finishing at a point just in front of the yarn post.

STEP 7

Tie in a very sparse clump of Z-Lon yarn for the spent wings. As a good rule of thumb, select the density that you think is appropriate, and then divide it in half. Lay it in just behind the upright post, and figure-eight it into place, so the yarn lies straight out to the sides of the hook.

STEP 9

Choose a high-quality dry-fly hackle. Strip the fibers from the bottom of the stem and tie it in just in front of the wing post. The hackle should be slightly undersized (when wrapped, the fibers should reach just to where the tail and biot meet), and tied in "shiny side up."

STEP 10

Winding the hackle in a clockwise direction, take three evenly spaced wraps up the post, then three more as you descend. Capture the hackle stem against the hook shank just in front of the thorax, with three to four tight wraps of thread, then clip off the excess hackle.

STEP 11

Trim any messy hackle fibers sticking out of the hook eye area, wind a few more cosmetic wraps, and whip-finish. Clip the yarn wing post to size. Its length, from where it exits the dubbed thorax to the top where you trim it, should be approximately the same length as the hook shank. You can vary this post length according to personal preference.

Most of the trout rose with surprising predictability, usually at 6- to 10-second intervals, presumably the amount of time it took to slide a gob of bugs down the gullet and then go back for seconds. Putting my fly over the fish at just that opportune moment increased the odds of hook-up substantially.

Dry flies are fished on Fall River with exclusively downstream presentations: casting above rising fish and feeding slack line onto the slow currents so that the first thing the trout sees is the fly, not the leader. The trick is to feed enough line into the system to achieve an absolutely drag-free presentation, without having so much slack as to make setting the hook difficult. Choosing the largest pair of lips I could see, I made a good slack-line cast above them, and watched as my perfect little downwing landed in a sea of look-alikes. *Uh-oh.* Houston, we have a problem. Which was my fly? Did it just get eaten, or was that a natural an inch to the side? Should I strike? My God, this was like some sort of Where's Waldo from Hell!

I hackle my *Callibaetis* Profile Spinner more lightly, as it will invariably be fished on lakes and sedate spring creeks.

Uh-oh. Houston, we have a problem. Which was my fly? Did it just get eaten, or was that a natural an inch to the side? Should I strike? My God, this was like some sort of Where's Waldo from Hell!

Okay, I reassured myself, *I can do this. I'm a professional guide. I know all the secrets, remember?* For the next two hours, however, the duration of the spinner fall, I resembled something more like a professional incompetent. Attempts to drag my pattern into a fish's lane, thereby allowing me to initially pick out my fly by its skating V-wake, failed utterly, as even the smallest drag resulted in the instantaneous attachment of a squadron of naturals to the counterfeit. Despite my hopes to the contrary, a clump of juicy naturals plastered to my impostor did not impress the trout. Basically—and to my utter chagrin—I

STEP 12

The finished Pale Morning Dun Profile Spinner as it looks to the tier…

came to the realization that I did not have an answer to this challenge. Here were hundreds of voracious, surface-feeding trout, eating a known fly, an insect I could replicate with a pattern they would take unhesitatingly, but the only hookups I achieved were largely accidents—either total "guess" strikes or, worse yet, fish I hooked while picking up line for the next cast (not that anyone else had to know about that one, mind you).

The problem was simply one of vision. Nearly invisible in the best of conditions, down-winged spinner patterns become virtually undetectable with: A) lots of competing naturals on the water; B) lots of naturals *and* tons of nerve-wracking rising fish in the water; and C) any semblance of a riffle on the water's surface. For once, here was a case where presentation wasn't the only key to success. For once, I had a chance to prove my theory that specificity of pattern can be just as important, in certain situations. And I knew I couldn't be the only one who felt this way.

Green Drake Profile Spinner, dressed heavily for choppy flows, but equally effective on flat water.

For once, here was a case where presentation wasn't the only key to success. For once, I had a chance to prove my theory that specificity of pattern can be just as important, in certain particular situations.

STEP 13

…and to the trout! Note the wispy, crumpled look of the spent wings, the delicate, realistic silhouette of the body, and how the hi-vis wing post so important to the angler is virtually invisible to the fish.

Okay, a show of hands: How many of you out there can no longer see well enough to tie on a new fly after the sun goes down? How about trying to pick out your size 18 Parachute Adams on late-afternoon water that's turned to total white-sheet glare? Is there anything worse than trying to see a spent-spinner pattern, lying flush in the surface film, as it runs a gauntlet of greedily slurping trout? If your eyes are aging as quickly as mine, you know there's nothing graceful about the process; for me the prospect of fishing a spinner fall had, until recently, come to have all the allure of chronic kidney stones.

Sure, I know all the tricks: lifting the rod tip, skating the fly a bit to find it on the water before starting the drift, using a tiny indicator a foot above the spinner, or—my favorite—strike everything. But the fact is, none of these techniques actually allows me to see my fly on the water. Fishing "blind" in this situation sucks the confidence right out of me, and when it comes to consistent success, confidence is the name of the game.

(My good friend and master tier Kelly Galloup ties a different pattern, in which he bends a gentle sideways curve into the hook to imitate the often-contorted body of the naturals. It's a neat trick you serious tiers might want to experiment with on this pattern as well. Just don't bend too much or you'll ruin the hook.)

The choice of thread was equally simple: I've come to use 8/0 UNI on almost all of my flies smaller than size 8 or 10, because there are so many colors and the tiny

If your eyes are aging as quickly as mine, you know there's nothing graceful about the process; for me the prospect of fishing a spinner fall had, until recently, come to have all the allure of chronic kidney stones.

"But vision problems are just part of the game," I can hear you arguing, "something we all have to learn to live with." Sorry, but in this case I disagree. I still believe in the possibility of "conditional magic flies," and in this situation, one existed. I set about to design it after my humiliation on the river that day, and this is how it came to be.

Any time I set out to design something new in flies, I start from scratch. What hook will best suit the creature I'm trying to emulate? In this case, the answer was easy: the standard-length dry-fly-model Tiemco would do nicely.

diameter amounts to almost no bulky buildup. Here, the camel color perfectly matched the rusty abdomen and thorax I wanted to tie. Many tiers like to use synthetic tailing fibers, like the popular Microfibetts, and understandably so. They are somewhat translucent, which the majority of actual mayfly tails are as well, and the synthetic perfection of each fiber makes them relatively easy to work with. They also come in a variety of colors to match almost any insect.

So I decided against them. Why? Two reasons. First, I believe synthetic tailing is a bit stiffer than real hackle fibers, and that a trout subtly nosing up to a pattern tied with it is more likely to push it away with its gentle rise-form, particularly if the tail is tied long and in the popular splayed profile. Second, as much as I use synthetics, something about these fibers just leaves me cold, used as described (although I do use them in a couple of nymphs, where they work fabulously). Not too scientific, I know— I've just learned to go with my experience and gut reaction sometimes.

One of the most perfect features of the spinner imitation I was using on Fall River was the turkey biot abdomen. Side by side with a natural, it would be difficult for the casual observer to see the difference, so beautifully and delicately segmented is the appearance, so naturally glossy the complexion this material lends to the fly. So I saw no reason to change this. It had consistently done well enough in less challenging circumstances, and I'd never seen a body material that looked better.

dark-dun wing color covers most species well enough to satisfy me. I believe the translucency, sheen and natural body of this material are far more important than the specific color. Best of all, it's durable and extremely easy to use.

One important tip: Keep the wings sparse. Better to have the wings more a *suggestion* than a heavy clump of fibers. Remember that the wings of real mayfly spinners are almost invisibly transparent, and often crumpled and imperfect in appearance. What is often thought of as a perfect silhouette can actually be too solid; a gauzy, suggestive look is preferable.

"Okay," you might say, "that's all well and good, but how is this design going to help me see my fly any better on the water?"

I'm glad you asked, because this is where the real secrets of the pattern start shining. First and most important, I decided the fly needed an upright posted wing—

> ## Keep the wings sparse. Better to have the wings more a *suggestion* than a heavy clump of fibers. Remember that the wings of real mayfly spinners are almost invisibly transparent, and often crumpled and imperfect in appearance.

Mahogany coloration is an excellent choice when diminutive *Paraleps* or smaller pale morning duns are emerging.

Over the years, the variety of materials used to construct spinner wings has been impressive. Polypropylene yarn was popular back in the 1970s and '80s, a period of much fly-tying innovation. Since then, cut-wing tools, hackle stems, hen feathers, trimmed hackle, foam and even bridal-veil material have contributed to the advances. Though I harbor a secret lust for hen-wing spinners, I rarely use them. They are difficult to tie correctly, and even when done right often twist a light tippet when casting. I keep a few of these delicate beauties— along with some of René Harrop's No-Hackles—in the box, for when I absolutely must catch a special fish. But my box is filled with spinners winged with Z-Lon. Dun or

without this bright indicator sticking well up above the surface of the water, nothing would allow me to easily pick my fly out of a crowd or in tough, glaring conditions. And if an indicator is what you're looking for, what better material to use than macramé indicator yarn? It's the same substance many "puffball" nymphing indicators are constructed of. There is no tying material I know with macramé yarn's unique combination of bulk (while still allowing for a very sparse tie-down area), buoyancy (remember, this stuff is employed to hold up split-shot!) and color (a trip to your local fly shop or craft store will produce it in whatever shocking neon hues your eyes can best see on the water).

Regarding the color, I suggest using a two-tone approach. I normally use a wing post that's a combination of hot-orange and bright-yellow fibers. This pairing covers a number of potentially challenging light situations, showing up equally well in white and dark glares. A simple black/white combo is another excellent choice. You can experiment to see what works best for you.

What are the downfalls of this very un-spinner-like appendage? Absolutely none. With the post tied in directly above the spent wings, there is no problem with balance, and I believe fish sometimes eat this pattern for a crippled dun, considering its multiple-wing silhouettes. Unlike some natural hairs, the yarn is simple to tie in and trim to length. It doesn't require tedious stacking techniques. Most important, it allows you to tie the same wonderfully sparse, realistic and productive spinner pattern that fish have always loved, only now you'll actually get to see them eat it!

To maintain a realistic body profile, I next used a very fine dubbing to form a thorax—larger in diameter than the abdomen, but not by much. Conveniently, the dubbing also helps to lock the spent wings into place.

Trico Profile Spinner—summertime trout candy.

Finally, I added a parachute hackle. Like the post, this is certainly not traditional for a spinner, but it adds a lot of buoyancy to the fly, with no drawbacks. Most people would never even consider fishing a spinner in broken water. As hard as they are to spot on flat water, seeing them in rough, choppy currents would be like shooting skeet in the dark. But do you think spinners exist only in slow pools? Of course not. During heavy spinnerfalls, bouncy riffles are normally loaded with dead and dying mayflies, and fish gorge there. Interestingly, this is often the water where they drown, or at least sink lower in the surface film. By applying floatant to the wing and parachute hackle only, Profile Spinners will accurately imitate this "reverse emergence" suspension profile.

Undoubtedly, trout also take this drift style as a crippled emerger or dun. In fact, this dry fly is quickly becoming my "go-to" pattern when searching broken water for random risers. They are particularly effective when afternoon thundershowers pound duns and spinners alike back down onto the water's surface.

Significantly, the hackle has proven wonderful on slick water, as well. I believe it forces the spent wings to suspend at just the right level, perhaps imitates legs, and definitely improves visibility to the angler while duping even the most discerning chalk-stream sippers.

Spinner falls are among the most visually arresting fly-fishing phenomena we experience. Watching these intense feeding orgies, with their accompanying acoustics of slurps and smacks, I never fail to feel the familiar catch of excitement, the thrill of anticipation that surface-feeding trout always instill in me. And now, for the first time, I approach them not with ambivalence, but rather with the same assurance I experience knotting a no-hackle dry to my 6X tippet when I really need to hook a fish.

Profile Spinners are as much a tying style as anything. I readily substitute foam bodies on huge Hexes, stack parachute hackling on drakes that need to float well in the heaviest of flows, and even make anatomical changes in creating versions for various caddisfly spentwings. I'm sure there are plenty of applications yet to be discovered. For now, though, I'm just happy to add one more "magic" fly to my box, one more wisp of confidence to pull out when I need it most.

Highly buoyant, realistic, extended foam-bodied Profile Spinners, Green Drake (top) and Hexagenia (bottom).

RAG SCULPIN

STREAMER FANATICS ARE AN ODD LOT. Take my friend John Dietz, for example. Show him a green drake hatch on the Henry's Fork and he reaches for a Zonker. PMDs on a spring creek? He sees leeches. One blustery spring day on the Madison not long back, with petite blue-winged olives stippling the water's surface, John knotted on a size 2 Woolhead Sculpin.

Is he nuts? Well, yes, he is. In a good sort of way. And he was also right. An open mind is a beautiful thing—it's worth noting that while I was struggling to dupe a handful of middling-sized rainbows rising to those tiny March sailboats, John was having the time of his life with trout of all proportions savaging his fast-twitched retrieve.

But, you counter, *fishing dry flies is so much more enjoyable, and civilized.* Yeah, whatever. That's what I was telling myself, too, right up until I had to stop and photograph John's sixth fish measuring greater than 18 inches. It didn't take much to figure who was having the most fun here. Dry-fly purity was beginning to appear grossly overrated.

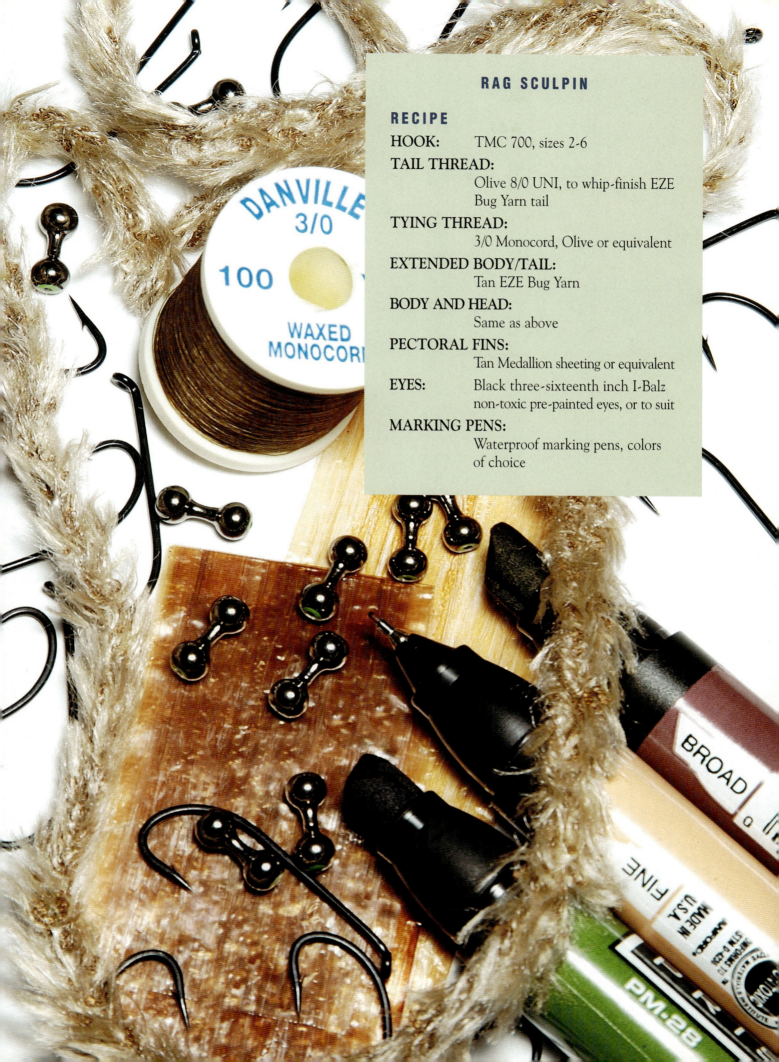

RAG SCULPIN

RECIPE

HOOK: TMC 700, sizes 2-6

TAIL THREAD:
Olive 8/0 UNI, to whip-finish EZE Bug Yarn tail

TYING THREAD:
3/0 Monocord, Olive or equivalent

EXTENDED BODY/TAIL:
Tan EZE Bug Yarn

BODY AND HEAD:
Same as above

PECTORAL FINS:
Tan Medallion sheeting or equivalent

EYES:
Black three-sixteenth inch I-Balz non-toxic pre-painted eyes, or to suit

MARKING PENS:
Waterproof marking pens, colors of choice

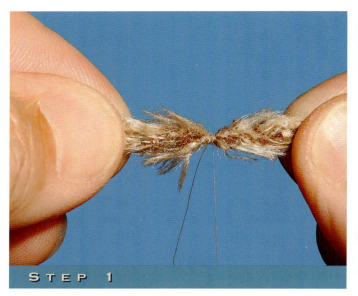

STEP 1

Cut a piece of EZE Bug yarn, six or seven inches in length. About half an inch from one end of the yarn, peel the fibers apart to expose the braided cores; with each end of the yarn held between separate fingers on either hand, use your bobbin to make six to 10 wraps of thread in this small area. It takes a little practice—once you get a couple of wraps in place you can release the bobbin, and just twirl the remaining wraps using centrifugal force. Use a hand whip finish to tie off. A drop of Flexament will help lock the thread wraps in place.

STEP 2

Just past the tie-down area, trim the end of the EZE Bug Yarn into a rounded shape, emulating the tail of an actual sculpin.

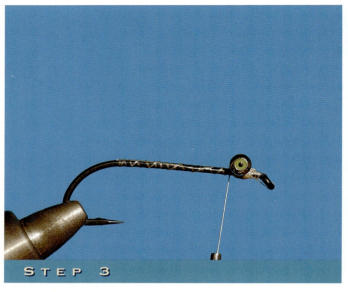

STEP 3

Wrap a thread base onto your hook shank, then figure-eight the I-Balz on at a point approximately one eye-length behind the hook eye.

STEP 4

The entire tail segment, from where it is attached to the hook just forward of the bend, to its rounded tip, should be about the same length as the hook shank. Spread the fibers apart at this point, exposing the braided core. Tie the yarn in at this core area, as it will reduce bulk and allow for a smooth-appearing transition between the tail and body. Really crank down tight on the thread here—if you don't secure the yarn well enough, the tail assembly will twist as you wrap the body. Note that the tail should be attached on a vertical plane, to give the fish a distinct and accurate profile when they view the fly from the side. It also encourages the tail to "swim" from side to side, a desirable trait.

STEP 5

To form the body, start wrapping the yarn forward. Just as you would when wrapping a body from Estaz, you'll want to take a wrap, then stroke the fibers back before making the next turn—this will avoid wrapping a lot of protruding fibers down.

STEP 6

When you reach a point about one hook-eye length behind the I-Balz, take several wraps around the yarn to secure it in place, then let it hang.

Tying a fly only slightly smaller than your average wharf rat to a leader you could use to trim your sidewalks with takes a huge leap of faith, especially when you're casting into familiar home water. After all, you know what these fish like. You've seen them refuse a dry because the 5X tippet looked like cable. Day in and day out, you've watched as they slurp tiny insects from the water's surface; repeated stomach pump samplings have confirmed their affinity for a variety of undersized bottom critters.

What you don't know, however, is that sculpins won't fit into those mini turkey-basters. They do slip down a trout's throat like cheesecake at Christmas dinner, though, and are just as highly prized. I have yet to find a stream with a healthy population of these homely baitfish that didn't support a trophy trout fishery to match.

Egg-sucking Rag Sculpin, deadly Alaskan and all-around version of the original, works best where salmon spawn.

One of my earliest recollections of the importance of sculpins came more than 20 years ago on Montana's then-sleeper fishery, the Beaverhead. Having long heard of the many huge browns lurking under the river's banks, I was amazed to find the stream was actually quite small, easily waded in many spots. Why, I asked myself, would such an undersized creek support such a large number of trophy trout? Two days later, I was a believer in the Beaverhead, having caught many 18- to 22-inch fish on a mixture of dries and nymphs, and losing a few true monsters on streamers—but I still couldn't explain the disproportionate population of outsized trout.

I got my answer the very next day when, for irrigation purposes, the stream's flows were suddenly and dramatically reduced. The river's main flow had been reduced by half. In just a matter of minutes, there were puddles of water left high and dry everywhere. Concerned the catastrophic drop might've stranded trout, I began wading through the ankle-deep pools, net in hand, ready to repatriate any unfortunate victims. Thirty minutes of fruitless searching later, I realized the Beaverhead trout must be accustomed to these violent fluctuations—not a single fish had been trapped. Something else, though, had not been so fortunate.

STEP 7

To create the sculpin's pronounced pectoral fins, fold a strip of Medallion sheeting over on itself (picture folding a bookmark in the middle so that both ends touch each other. Yes, this IS important; folded lengthwise, the formed pectorals will shred just being tied in). Beginning at the fold, cut straight up a short distance, then form a round "balloon," finishing with another short, straight cut as you once again cut through the fold. The finished product should look like a round ball with a square peg sticking out one end. Cut this way, you've also created two identical pectorals, kind of like the paper dolls idea. Separate them by cutting the material at the only place it's connected, at the fold.

STEP 8

Tie one on the near side first, using the short little "peg" as a tie-down mechanism, then repeat the process on the far side. The pectorals, if pressed back against the body, should reach nearly to the point of the hook, and be at least as tall as the body of the sculpin is, from back to belly.

STEP 9

The next wrap or two of yarn needs to be behind the pectorals, to force them to flare straight out.

STEP 10

As you complete the wrap(s) behind the pectorals, feed the yarn between the gap at the bottom of the fins, to bring it forward. Now take two or three wraps of the yarn between the pectorals and the I-Balz, to build the necessary bulk to emulate the wide, flattened "catfish" head profile desired. Make a single figure-eight of the yarn around the eyes, then tie it down immediately in front of them.

STEP 11

Whip-finish and trim the thread.

Note the oversized pectorals tied correctly. These will alternately protrude and flatten against the body, depending on the current or the speed of your retrieve.

STEP 12

Use your scissors to trim the top and bottom of the head, accentuating the "shovelhead" look. Also, trim the entire belly beneath the hook shank and the back of the fly, so that the body and the tail silhouettes flow together. Finally, trim some but not all of the yarn bulk away from the base of the pectorals—note that there are short, trimmed fibers left both in front of and behind the fins, which serve to support them in a partially flared position. They'll lay against the body when the fly is stripped against a current, then pop back out when it comes to rest.

Sculpins. Thousands of them, actually—so thick in some places that a well-scooped net came up heavy with writhing masses of the lizard-like little fish. I was starting to get the picture.

Now, I'm not saying that I impaled a few of these squirmy baitfish onto a nymph hook (though I would have lip-hooked them, if I had) and tossed them into the nearby stream (just as a scientific experiment), but rest assured they were immediately engulfed in massive boils (er, I mean they would have been, had I actually carried through with the fleeting thought), followed by short, brutal surges and severely compromised tippets. *Screw the nymphs*, I remember thinking, *these fish want meat!* As it happens, my fraudulent baitfish weren't quite so irresistible to the big carnivores, but I'd seen enough to ignite my interest—now a lifelong passion—for tying and fishing sculpin patterns.

A few notes regarding sculpins:

1. They are appallingly unattractive. If they grew to the size of salmon, wet wading would be a thing of the past, and Simms would be making armored, not breathable, waders.

2. For all intents and purposes, they are without scales. This gives them a texture like slimy leather, which trout for some reason seem to find ravenously appealing.

3. They have no swim bladder. This means they are destined to eternal exile as bottom-dwellers, which is actually a pretty good thing for a sculpin because, as with trout, a majority of the sculpin's diet consists of aquatic insects found in and around streambed rocks. They tend to move in short, erratic bursts, rarely swimming for any distance.

4. Their compressed, flattened body profile, tapering to a narrow tail, is perfectly adapted, hydrodynamically, to foraging the bottom in mild to heavy flows. Even the sculpin's fanlike pectorals aid in gripping bottom structure.

5. Sculpins seem to have a chameleon-like ability to blend in with the color of the substrate they live on. I've observed variations of brown, olive, black, tan, rust, and gold, and most are mottled, completing the camouflage

STEP 13

The fully trimmed fly, viewed from above.

STEP 15

The finished Rag Sculpin.

STEP 14

Using an olive waterproof marking pen, color the entire top 180 degrees of the sculpin, being careful to keep the belly the realistic creamy shade of the yarn. Color all of the pectorals, front and back. Repeat this process with a dark brown pen, but just mottle the yarn this time, so that the sculpin has the splotchy, muddy olive/brown look of the real thing. You can, of course, vary the coloration of your sculpin to taste, or the actual hue of local specimens.

effect. Though their bellies are quite often light-colored, they are virtually invisible from above, unless they move. They routinely inhabit lakes, as well as moving water, a fact most stillwater anglers seem unaware of. A major oversight.

For years, I've felt there's been a dearth of practical, well-designed, great-fishing sculpin patterns. Many superb general-purpose streamers are probably taken for sculpins—Zonkers and Woolly Buggers among these—but don't specifically try to emulate them. Mike Lawson, one of our country's finest tiers and anglers, gave us the venerable Woolhead Sculpin some years back. The pattern has become the sculpin of choice for most serious streamer fishers, from Alaska to Argentina. Deservedly so, as it matches most of the above attributes amazingly well.

To its credit, the Woolhead's uncomplicated yet well-thought-out design has made it a favorite "guide fly," a designation most tying innovators recognize as high praise, an honor bestowed on patterns relatively easy to tie that have stood the test of time. For years, my friend John fished it nearly to the exclusion of all others. It has a good profile, and the materials used are absorbent, keeping it from planing to the surface of the water when fished on a floating line. I, unfortunately, am cursed with a character flaw that always imagines a better, magic fly is out there, productive beyond imagination, ready to be discovered if only one can find the right combination of materials and form.

In the coming chapter about my Rag Hex Nymph, I've written of the late Hugh Beglin's wonderful discovery and development of EZE Bug Yarn, a material perfectly suited to large-fly construction. In fact, with the very first samples Hugh sent me, he included a sculpin of his own design, in his words just a quick sample to show possible applications of the material. The moment I saw his pattern,

I knew he was onto something remarkable: Here was a single material that built bulk quickly, could be trimmed to shape, possessed an integral mottling, took coloring from marking pens well, and soaked up and held water beautifully. The applications were unlimited. So it was, with this material as a foundation, that I began my venture to create a lifelike sculpin pattern that fish would find irresistible.

Trout are used to seeing sculpins on the bottom, often nearly motionless, and usually by themselves. Not darting about in schools, not holding mid-depth in a current, and not cruising around endlessly in the shallows. On the bottom. For this, I wanted a very specific hook: one that

black, down-turned-eye, salmon and steelhead iron strong enough to tow a Buick, and retaining Tiemco's trademark razor sharpness without the tendency to distort. Perfect.

Despite its apparent bulk, EZE Bug is composed of three thread-like cores twisted together, each with long fibers extending outward. Since you're always tying just the relatively slender cords down, not the bulky mass of the fibers, you can get away with using moderately small thread—8/0, if you're careful, though I find 3/0 more appropriate when it's necessary to bind the material down securely. As for thread color, simply match the finished body color of the fly.

A deadly duo that haunts fish dreams. The egg-sucking variation is lethal when dead-drifted to trout lying behind spawning salmon. Fish the standard Rag Sculpin on a sinking-tip line, twitching it slowly through deep runs.

would sink quickly just by virtue of its wire weight; be heavy enough to keep its point intact in spite of the constant bottom-banging it would endure; have adequate shank length to incorporate the actual sculpin's body profile; and be strong enough to let me really lean on a big fish in heavy currents.

My first attempts were on the TMC 5263, that wonderful, 3X long streamer/nymph model that has been the chassis of so many respected large trout flies. Though a pretty good choice, I found it had an annoying flaw, for my use—when dragged across enough stony bottoms, the very tip of the hook point would eventually bend out. Digging deeper into my box of hooks (literally—I'm so unorganized that I keep all of my hook back-stock in a tattered old shoebox), I "rediscovered" the TMC 700, a

Almost all of the patterns I tie using EZE Bug are of the extended body style; it's a natural application, given the material's realistic appearance and supple motion when wet. To make this work, you must first realize that the twisted cores, when wet, untwist, leaving you with a tail or abdomen appearing to be, well, untwisted. To overcome this, make eight to 10 wraps of thread around the twisted cores, near one end of the piece being used, then whip-finish off in the same place.

Though I don't bother, you could also dab a drop of head cement or super glue onto the thread, just to insure against knot failure. With the Rag Sculpin, I leave a short length of EZE Bug behind the tie-down, and then trim it into a rounded shape, a dead-ringer for the tapered-yet-blunt silhouette of the natural's tail.

Look carefully at EZE Bug and you will see that it has a flattened profile (the fibers tend to stick out at a right angle to the core, not unlike hackle fibers off a hackle stem), with the core giving the material a three-dimensional bulk in the middle that perfectly emulates the rearward anatomy of a sculpin, or most any baitfish. I tie the tail assembly in (it should be approximately the same length as the hook shank) so the fibers point up and down, giving predators a full, wide outline viewed from the side, or narrower contour if spotted from above.

After attaching the tail, I begin winding the yarn forward, just as you would Hugh's other brainchild, Estaz. You take a wrap, use your free hand to comb the fibers back toward the tail (and hold them there), then wrap again. Repeat until you've covered approximately two-thirds of the shank. This gives a smooth, solid body with all the fibers lying back uniformly, and avoids the messy look created when you simply and quickly wrap forward, tying down many fibers. It's a small trick, but gives a much better finished product. At this point, I take a couple of securing wraps behind the yarn to hold it in place, and let it hang while I prepare the pectorals.

An alternate tie with a slimmer-profile body. In streams with light-colored substrate, resident, bottom-dwelling sculpins are mottled in complementary shades.

A sculpin has pectoral fins like an elephant has ears—not exactly outsized for the animal, but they sure draw your attention. I believe trout recognize this characteristic, as it is so different from the fin structure of other baitfish. As I always say, never pass up the chance to design in a good triggering feature. The pectorals are alternately splayed out or flattened against the sculpin's body, and are semi-translucent—mottled, but vaguely transparent.

Two things bothered me about the opaque feathers often used for these fins on other patterns. First, most were solid in color and did not appear realistic to me (partridge feathers have a beautiful natural mottling, but are nearly impossible to find in the correct colors). Second, these feathers were sometimes a bit rigid, causing the fly to plane unnaturally in the water when retrieved.

I finally settled on a material called Medallion. It has a milky, diaphanous quality, just the right amount of rigidity (Medallion pectorals fold against the body when cast or

pulled against a current, but pop out slightly when resting on the bottom), and take a marking pen perfectly. I find that when I form the pectoral fins out of this material, it's best to cut with the grain, as it reduces splitting of the sheeting. Also, always err on the side of making them too large—you can always whittle them down later, if needed. I like to make the cut round for the actual fin, and leave a short tab at one end for ease of tying in. As a final tip, to make sure your pectorals are all similar in size, I suggest folding the material over several times, then cut one outline. Presto, just like paper dolls!

If there is one feature most associated with the sculpin, it's the head. Interestingly, the head is flattened, like the tail, but on an opposite plane, reminiscent of a catfish. Compressed and wide, with fleshy lips, and eyeballs that only a gecko could love—the word that comes immediately to mind is toady. To aid in mimicking this reptilian visage, I use heavy non-toxic painted dumbbell eyes, as they just look right, help achieve a plummeting sink rate, and provide the perfect framework with which to form a widened cranial silhouette. The placement of the eyes is crucial—too far forward, you won't have room to tie off the fly; too far back, and you'll end up with a skinny "nose." I imagine the shank space needed to achieve a single revolution of EZE Bug, and tie the eyes in that far behind the hook eye. Likewise, there should be enough width for one wrap of the yarn between the pectorals and the eyes.

Once the pectorals and eyes are in place, begin wrapping the yarn forward again, starting with a revolution or two behind the pectorals. This builds appropriate bulk and forces the fins to stand out from the body more prominently. (They'll still collapse against the body when cast or retrieved, but they'll remain slightly flared when at rest.) Finish this revolution with the yarn underneath the hook so you don't mash the fins as you wrap in front of them.

The first wrap in front will lay the fins back slightly, but not so much that they're forced to lie flat against the body. The second wrap, still behind the eyes, will basically lie on top of the first one, providing the graduation in bulk to support the next step. You can even take a third wrap here, if space allows. To cover the eye tie-down area, you'll want to figure-eight the yarn between the terminal ends of the eyes; on a smaller sculpin a single figure eight is normally sufficient, while you may want to double the procedure on a size 2 or larger hook. If you placed the eyes correctly, there will now be just a small area of shank left behind the hook eye; not enough for another wrap of yarn, but sufficient space to comfortably tie off.

At this point, you should have an excellent semblance of a sculpin, albeit with a rather unruly-looking head. Using a pair of sharp, straight-bladed scissors, trim the yarn flat on the underside of the head—this should make the entire bottom of the fly fairly even. Do basically the same on top of the head, though instead of a flat cut, trim a slightly rounded profile, starting flush with the hook at the eye, tapering up so that at a point just behind the eyes the head and back fibers are the same length.

Typically, there will be fibers nearly obscuring the front face of the pectorals—I like to trim these down so that 80 to 90 percent of the fins are showing. Also, you may want to shorten the fibers behind the pectorals just for aesthetic purposes; do not cut away any of the bulk near the base of the fins here, though, as this is what supports and pushes them outwards.

Your Rag Sculpin is nearly complete. In fact, if you chose to use a darker color yarn, you may decide to call it good at this point. Personally, keeping in mind how mottled actual sculpins are—and how readily EZE Bug will absorb waterproof marking pens—I like to add a final step of coloring.

I usually tie my sculpins with tan yarn: It makes a great blank canvas. Remember that the fly's belly should

stream, make a large initial mend (upstream if in a heavy current, down if in slower flows), then drop the rod and pulse the tip repeatedly in the direction of the mend. Enough to make the fly dart several inches, but not so violently as to introduce significant slack into my line.

On streams with lighter colored substraits the resident sculpins are modeled accordingly. Note the alternate, slimmer body profile that some anglers prefer.

A few notes regarding sculpins:
1. They are appallingly unattractive. If they grew to the size of salmon, wet wading would be a thing of the past, and Simms would be making armored, not breathable, waders.

remain light-colored; as you apply color, take care to avoid the underside. Begin with the lightest color you'll be using, smudging it over about 75 percent of the fly. Follow this with the next, darker shade, covering the remaining 25 percent, plus a bit of overlap. Finally, if you choose to use a third color, do so very sparingly (it's definitely possible to have too much of a good thing). As an example, my standard sculpin has a base of olive, mottled over with dark brown, with eight to 10 small black spots (about twice the size of a pencil eraser, but irregularly shaped). Some sculpins have distinct banding across their backs—you might color up a few with these, just to experiment. When fished, the colors tend to run together a bit, which I like. If some bleeds into the belly, don't worry—it'll still be much lighter than the top, and that's all that really matters. Be sure to use all of the colors on the pectorals, as well.

To be honest, much streamer fishing, done right, is a lot of work. Expect a sore neck from casting large flies, and aching shoulders from hours of mending and aggressive line stripping. For most anglers, it will never be their go-to method, just another rabbit to pull out of the hat when hunting big trout. Done right, though—and trust me, it's not brain surgery—it is an exciting new addition to your stable of techniques. I rarely pull streamers all day. I prefer to increase my odds of success by concentrating on periods of low light when big trout are likely to be on the prowl: mornings, evenings and inclement weather.

With the Rag Sculpin, I'll often simply cast across

It's amazing how subtly and quickly a fish can take and then reject such a large bite. Under the best of conditions, I'll miss a high percentage of the grabs I get. For this reason, I usually slowly strip in line as I work the fly with the rod, in an attempt to stay tight to the fly. Remember, strikes are free—set the hook at the slightest hesitation in the drift, or if you detect an unusual weight or drag on your line. Odds are, the fly is in a trout's maw! If the water is slow, I'll switch to a more conventional cast-and-retrieve technique, making sure my rod tip is on or slightly under the water's surface. Again, no two-foot-long strips—that's not how sculpins move. I prefer an erratic presentation, interspersing short two- to four-inch spurts with equally short slow pulls—just enough to keep tension on the line.

Be prepared—any grab you get when fishing this fly is likely to come from a substantial beast!

MICRO MAYFLY NYMPH

"WELL, IT'S…DIFFERENT. IN A GOOD WAY, I MEAN. Sorta… different."

I wasn't exactly overwhelmed with this praise for my new invention: a fly I was certain would become the next Gold Bead Prince Nymph.

"No, really, I like it. I've never seen anything quite—quite like it."

Jim Murphy was actually the first person to whom I'd shown my new pattern. We were sitting slouched forward, lounging on a pair of streamside boulders on the banks of Montana's Madison River. The afternoon was an unseasonable 95°Fahrenheit, and the normally productive river had been particularly unkind to us. Not a fish showed itself anywhere; dry flies had given way to nymphs, nymphs to despair. Our confidence was shot.

MICRO MAYFLY NYMPH

RECIPE

HOOK: TMC 921 or TMC 3769, sizes 14-18

THREAD: 8/0 UNI, color to match fly

TAIL: Three ringneck pheasant tail fibers (dyed yellow for olive fly, natural copper for brown version)

RIB: Fine silver wire

ABDOMEN: Stripped peacock herl

WING CASE "STRIPE":
Strand of pearl Flashabou

WING CASE: Dark golden-brown turkey tail

THORAX: Mercer's Select Buggy Nymph Dubbing, Micro May color, or to preference

LEGS: Same as tail

EPOXY: Devcon 5 Minute Epoxy or equivalent

COLLAR: Same as thorax

BEAD: Small copper bead

STEP 1

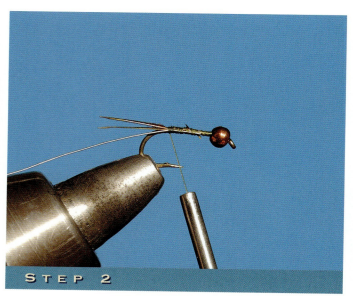

STEP 2

Slide a small copper bead on the hook all the way to the eye. Form a sparse base with your thread from the bead back to a point directly in front of the bend of the hook. Select three fibers from the thicker-fibered, copperish (recognizable even though the feather is dyed yellow) side of a ringneck pheasant tail feather, taken from the center of the entire tail splay. It's important to use these fibers, as the softer tan fibers found on the outside feathers typically won't separate and splay correctly. Use your fingers to make sure the fiber tips are aligned evenly, then pinch them to the top of the hook at a point just forward of the bend; tie them down. If there is thread in back of the feather tie-down spot, wrap the thread back over the fibers until you reach that original tie-down, while gently pulling the fibers back and upward. When you release the fibers, they should splay apart from each other slightly. If not, simply push them up from underneath with your thumbnail or the side of a scissor blade—this will accomplish the desired look. If you've ever watched a natural mayfly nymph resting in the water column between bursts of swimming, you've noticed how frequently it raises and splays its tails, presumably to keep from sinking back down. Wrap the fibers down to a point just behind the bead and trim off the excess.

Tie in the wire rib. To create a smooth underbelly, wrap the wire down along nearly the entire length of the hook shank.

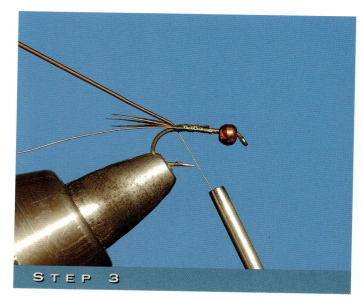

STEP 3

Using a pencil eraser, rub all the nap off a peacock herl. Tie in the remaining stem by its tip.

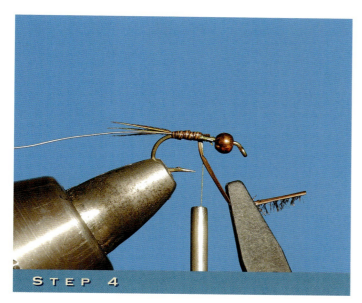

STEP 4

Grasp the stem with a pair of hackle pliers and wind forward, forming a quill body covering about half the available hook shank. Tie off and trim the excess.

STEP 5

Wrap the wire forward, creating an evenly spaced rib.

"I came up with this idea last year when we were here," I explained, watching as he turned it over in his fingers. "One day, there was a bunch of fish just above Three Dollar, in really shallow, fast water, eating tiny mayfly nymphs. I couldn't use a split-shot, because I hung up constantly, but all my nymphs that were the right size were too light—they just skimmed over the top of the fish. I decided to come up with a pattern that had a super-thin abdomen, just like the naturals, but would sink like a rock. You want a couple of these to try?"

"Sure. Can't hurt at this point."

Again, I was moved by his confidence. Putting my bruised ego aside, I knotted on one of the little anchors myself, and began working my way upstream.

For reasons that escape me, trout seem to find red wire-bodied Micro Mayflies absolutely delectable.

Then the funniest thing happened. It was like the fish had come back. With each indicator pull-down my confidence grew, every cartwheeling 16-inch rainbow convincing me I was on to something big.

Then the funniest thing happened. It was like the fish had come back. Every pocket I knew held fish, did. Every perfect drop riffle was good for at least two or three trout. A major run might produce half a dozen. With each indicator pull-down my confidence grew, every cartwheeling 16-inch rainbow convincing me I was on to something big. I wasn't using the nymph in the type of water I'd designed it for, but who cared? The fish everywhere seemed to love it! I couldn't wait to find Jim and see how he was faring.

Two hours later, still hammering fish and nearly hyperventilating with excitement over my new find, I rounded a corner and found Jim, his rod bucking to the headshakes of an obviously unamused rainbow. I got ready for his accolades about the new wonder fly.

"All right—that looks good. How's it been?"

"Terrible," he replied. "This is the first fish I've

STEP 6

Tie in a single strand of Flashabou, taking care to position it directly on top of the hook.

STEP 8

Repeat the previous step with another slip of turkey tail.

STEP 7

Tie in a slip of darkly mottled golden-brown turkey tail feather, securing it to the top of the hook shank.

STEP 9

Dub a thorax, using most of the remaining hook shank, making it slightly plumper than the abdomen.

Select three of the same type of pheasant-tail fibers as used in the tail, and make sure the tips are aligned. Tie the tips in immediately in front of and on the far side of the thorax. If pressed back against the body, they should reach a point just short of the rear of the abdomen. Trim the excess.

Repeat the process on the near side of the hook.

hooked in the last hour." (My heart sank: Was my success all just a fluke? Had I just been at the right place at the right time? Would any pattern have worked?) "But if you have any more of those goofy-looking little things left, I'd sure like some—until I broke them off, it was just stupid, they worked so well!"

And so, our newest "ultimate" confidence fly was born. It was what we reached for in every situation the rest of that day, and most of the remainder of the trip. Big, brawling rivers, tiny meadow rivulets, even in lakes with fish chasing *Callibaetis* nymphs; there was just something magical about the fly, something that triggered a feeding response time and time again.

A dark, glossy wing case perfectly mimics that of a natural emerging mayfly on its way to the surface.

> **Big, brawling rivers, tiny meadow rivulets, even in lakes with fish chasing *Callibaetis* nymphs; there was just something magical about the fly, something that triggered a feeding response time and time again.**

Was it the nymph's profile? Its unusual wing case? The way it gets immediately down to the trout's level? Those are good questions—let's consider them, and others.

My friend Cory Williams, a master angler, tier, and keen observer of Nature, is always preaching to me about the importance of slender profiles when it comes to designing smaller mayfly patterns.

"It isn't possible to tie a *Baetis* or PMD, nymph or adult, too sparsely," Cory exhorts. "Just turn over a river rock for a nymph, or scoop a floating dun off the water's surface. Look at it—in many cases, the actual body is more slender than any hook you can use!" Always one to practice what he preaches, Cory ties many of his wonderfully productive mayfly imitations using only thread for abdomens. While we don't always agree, I'm convinced Cory is right on the money with this one. It was with this credo in the back of my mind that I began the tying

STEP 12

Pull the first wing case forward over the thorax, tying it down directly behind the bead. Don't stretch it too tightly or the turkey strip will break into its individual fibers—not desirable, as it will allow the epoxy to seep through.

STEP 14

Pull the Flashabou "stripe" forward, directly over and down the middle of the wing case; tie it down and trim excess.

STEP 13

Repeat with the second strip.

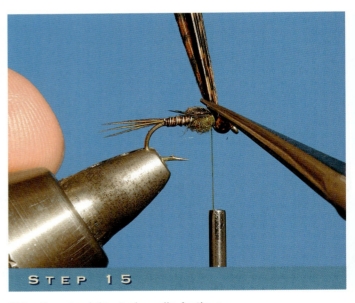

STEP 15

Trim the remaining turkey slip feathers.

STEP 16

Using a fine-tipped bodkin or needle, apply a thin coat of 5 Minute Epoxy to the wing case. Don't concern yourself with the thickness of the epoxy at this point—simply make sure you cover every bit of the feather. As soon as this is accomplished, and before the epoxy starts to harden, place another drop of the epoxy in the middle of the wing case; it will immediately self-level, giving you a beautiful, glossy effect. The size of this second drop will determine how thick or "high" the finished wing case will be.

STEP 17

Dub a short collar to hide the wing case tie-down area.

process for what would become the Micro Mayfly by making a rather unusual hook choice.

A Tiemco 921 is a dry-fly hook, short in length and not particularly stout of wire—attributes that might not immediately recommend it for use as a nymph. But they are exactly the features that prompted my choice. The designation as a dry-fly model meant almost nothing to me. I'd used the hook before. Knowing that most anglers would be using my creation with 4X, 5X or 6X tippets, I knew there was little concern regarding strength. What mattered was having a foundation that would allow me to create my perfect small mayfly nymph: short, skinny and with enough hook gape to accommodate the oversized bead I planned on using to maximize sink rate. I'd always appreciated the slightly exaggerated bend style of this hook, which seemed to maximize hooking success when used in its more traditional role as a parachute dry-fly base. Finally, I knew the slightly finer-wire hook would slip into a trout's jaw with less effort, improving hookup rates. (The TMC 3769 is also a good choice for this pattern.)

This Pheasant Tail Micro Mayfly tied with a tungsten bead sinks faster than a rock. Fish love the glint of wire.

"It isn't possible to tie a *Baetis* or PMD, nymph or adult, too sparsely," Cory exhorts. Always one to practice what he preaches, Cory ties many of his wonderfully productive mayfly imitations using only thread for abdomens.

I must have the world's largest collection of tying threads. Every time a new model comes on the market, I eagerly buy into the hype surrounding it ("The diameter of hair, yet doubles as a tow chain for yanking big rigs out of the mud"), usually only to find the product pretty much the same as every other brand. I have to admit, though, I've finally been largely persuaded away from my dependable old prewaxed 6/0, lured by the wide and well-thought-out color choices and tiny-yet-strong diameter of UNI's 8/0 line of threads.

When trying to minimize bulk in a pattern, choice of

STEP 18

The finished Micro Mayfly Nymph.

thread is my first line of attack. I find 8/0 the perfect "weight-watcher." As well, one must always consider how a thread color may "bleed" through whatever it's tying down, dubbed bodies in particular. Though I'm not as concerned with exact color matches as I am with marrying properly shaded hues (light-colored threads with light-colored bodies, etc.), the impressive range of pigments the UNI product comes in, particularly the wide array of earth tones, has won me over.

The choice of tailing material is absolutely crucial to a nymph's effectiveness, yet the step is often given all the rote attention of tying one's shoes. Considering that many mayfly nymphs use their tails and abdomens for movement—the very thing that often attracts a trout's attention—choosing a material or tying style to emulate this motion only makes sense. Many of the tiny mayfly species I wanted the Micro Mayflies to imitate have three tails, appendages they alternately close together and use as an extension of their abdomen to aid in swimming, then spread apart to retard their sink rate, when they take a rest. My challenge was to find a delicate, yet durable, slightly tapered fiber stiff enough to hold its splayed profile when sinking or dead-drifted, yet soft enough to collapse into a single silhouette when retrieved.

As of this writing, the brown Micro Mayfly has become my most popular pattern of all time. Boy, does it catch fish.

Sound like a ridiculous detail? Don't bet on it. Particularly on some of today's heavily pressured spring creeks, trout will routinely respond to a small visual accuracy like this, while refusing more heavily dressed conventional tailing styles.

Sound like a ridiculous detail? Don't bet on it. Particularly on some of today's heavily pressured spring creeks, trout will routinely respond to a small visual accuracy like this, while refusing more heavily dressed conventional tailing styles.

One final note: Tails tied too short will be stiff and

unresponsive in the water, while tails that are too long look unrealistic and can foul annoyingly on the hook. Try to keep the tail roughly the same length as the hook shank when tying the Micro Mayflies.

I believed the abdomen was a critical design stage for this pattern—it needed to be exceptionally slender and possess subtle but noticeable segmentation. I thought immediately of turkey biots, with their lifelike sheen and raised-edge banding, but this idea, like so many in creative

peacock herl. This material is quite flat and reflects a wonderfully subdued glow, even adding a slightly banded, segmented appearance to the fly. Frailty was its only real downfall, but adding a fine wire rib solved this problem, as well as allowing me to control the segmentation spiral without adding bulk. The wire actually even added a touch of sink rate. Interestingly, the abdomen is always the tying step I get questioned about—no one can ever figure out what the material is.

My gut tells me tying legs on such undersized imitations is a waste of effort. I like the way my gut thinks; my gut is my friend. Unfortunately, my traitorous brain reminds me I should never miss an opportunity to design in a possible feeding trigger. My brain, alas, is smarter than my gut.

tying, worked much better on paper than in practice. The segment edges were just too prominent for such a delicate project, and when the biot revolutions were made closely enough to each other to create accurate segmentation, they created undesirable bulk.

Next I thought of Cory and his thread bodies. When I tried this, however, I didn't get the "shine" I wanted to capture, based on live insect samples I'd observed (I have to admit, though, that they fished very well). Finally, looking at some chalk-stream patterns featured in a British tying magazine, I had my inspiration—stripped

Dubbing is wonderful stuff. You can use it to form giant bodies, or tiny heads, and everything in between. There is a color and style for any application, and when it gets wet, it glistens and gives the illusion of life. It was the obvious choice for the thorax on my new nymph, and I took it. As always, I made sure to use a product that used multiple colors to create one dominant one—much as, in music, three or more tones create a chord. I believe this increases the chance of a fish seeing a hue it likes. I made it a bit larger in diameter than the abdomen, but not much, as I wanted to maintain a relatively slim profile.

Ideally, the thorax should comprise approximately 40 to 50 percent of the entire fly's length, just as with the natural.

The wing case provides a critical key to this pattern's success—of that I have no doubt. At what stage are most small mayflies their most vulnerable and available to trout? Emergence, of course. From the moment they release their grip on the streambed cobble and begin the arduous trek to the surface, these tiny travelers are in the crosshairs of actively feeding fish. Specifically, what features are most pronounced in these emergers? I found the answer many years ago on the storied flats of Hat Creek, while observing massive hatches of pale morning duns. I was working on what would eventually become the Poxyback PMD nymph, doing daily seinings (back when it was still legal to do so here) and observations of the emerging nymphs.

My friend John Dietz suggested a chartreuse variation. I suspect fish sometimes take it for a small lime-colored caddisfly pupa.

Virtually all the little critters displayed classic dark wing cases, swollen and distended with trapped gas and fluid, easily the most pronounced symptom of impending emergence. I discovered then that a coat of 5 Minute Epoxy over a dark, feather wing case produced a superb counterfeit. Though I didn't pay enough attention to it at the time, a small percentage had begun to emerge underwater, their obsidian shoulders displaying a thin slit of brilliance as the wing case split, revealing a glimpse of the luminous insect beneath. I was reminded of this phenomenon years later, pumping the throats of some nymph-guzzling browns on a western tailwater. Remembering what I'd seen that day on Hat Creek, I realized it could be a significant feeding trigger.

I resolved to work on a solution. My first attempts centered on creating an actual split wing case. Obvious, right? These attempts were complex, multi-step, unqualified disasters. Beautiful in the vise, they exploded in the mouths of trout. Many failed attempts later, the Flashabou "stripe" (on top of the turkey-tail wing case, beneath the coat of epoxy) idea occurred to me, and I had my answer.

Different from the popular, gaudy flashback style of wing cases, this technique captures the glossy ballooning of the natural's trapped wings, with just a hint of a splitting skin. It works outrageously well. I've since incorporated the design into many other patterns.

My gut tells me tying legs on such undersized imitations is a waste of effort. After all, the miniature swimmers I've observed wiggling about in Petri dishes all seem to tuck their legs against their bodies while in motion. I like the way my gut thinks; my gut is my friend. Unfortunately, my traitorous brain reminds me I should never miss an opportunity to design in a possible feeding trigger. My brain tells me not to be such a lazy tier. My brain, alas, is smarter than my gut.

As it turns out, the same pheasant-tail fibers used for the Micro Mayfly's tail make great legs. They're durable, tapered, and soft enough to add slight movement to the drifting nymph. I like to tie them slightly longer than the length of the thorax. Are the legs critical to success? Questionable. Should you bother with this step? Wait a moment, while I consult again with my brain.

Invariably, tying down the turkey-tail wing case leaves a band of bare tying thread behind the metal bead. This bugs me. To alleviate the unfinished look, I apply a very sparse wrap of the same dubbing used in the thorax. Then, when I whip-finish just behind the bead, the locking wraps slide beneath the dubbing, effectively making them invisible.

> **At what stage are most small mayflies their most vulnerable and available to trout? Emergence, of course. From the moment they release their grip on the streambed cobble and begin the arduous trek to the surface, these tiny travelers are in the crosshairs of actively feeding fish.**

Remember, a fast sink-rate was one of the two main criteria I had for this pattern. So, instead of matching the small hook size with a correspondingly tiny bead, I upsized. Yes, it looks a bit goofy, but what beadhead pattern doesn't, really?

I can't imagine trout like beadheads because they actually resemble any part of a bug's anatomy—if fish are primarily attracted to the shine of a bead, a slight size difference won't make much difference. And the small increase in diameter adds up to a much faster-sinking fly. Perfect for use in the hopper/dropper setup so popular in the Rocky Mountain states, it's also one of the very few small nymphs that can penetrate water currents quickly enough to eliminate the need for a split shot or second, larger fly so commonly used for sink rate. In fact, its narrow silhouette and heavy bead are so adept at scouring stream bottoms, I often use it as my anchor pattern, usually in front of another small mayfly or midge pupa. When I use it as a single pattern in rough, heavy currents, I'll sometimes use variations with wire abdomens and/or tungsten beads; their extra flash is easier for trout to pick up in faster flows, and they're even heavier than the standard tie.

> **I'm always amazed how many people are hesitant to try these tiny mayfly nymphs, apparently concerned they won't be substantial enough to catch the attention of larger fish. In many tailwaters, trout survive by consuming vast amounts of these microscopic bonbons, lots of which are far punier than any possible artificial fly.**

As ardent fly fishers continue to flock to ice-cold tailwater rivers, the indigenous small-insect biomasses (*Baetis*, *Tricos*, midges, etc.) play progressively larger roles in those anglers' fly selections. It's been my experience that, with the exception of isolated seasonal emergences, trout in our high-pressured fisheries are much more aggressive toward small nymphs than large ones, often ignoring or spooking from anything above a size 16. I'm always amazed how many people are hesitant to try these tiny mayfly nymphs, apparently concerned they won't be substantial enough to catch the attention of larger fish. In fact, nothing could be further from the truth. In many tailwaters, trout survive by consuming vast amounts of these microscopic bonbons, lots of which are far punier than any possible artificial fly.

If you're skeptical, try this: Knot on your favorite larger nymph pattern normally, then run a foot-long piece of tippet off the bend of the hook. To the end of this tippet, tie on a Micro Mayfly, then go fish. I think you'll be surprised which fly gets all the attention!

ALASKA LEMMING

SLAMMED AWKWARDLY AND HEADLONG INTO THE FRIGID CURRENT, the reluctant swimmer was overwhelmed by a blinding rush of panic. Water invaded his nose and mouth, choking off all breath. As he clawed frantically at the terror, his head suddenly broke the surface, allowing great, ragged gasps of air and a brief opportunity to collect himself. Only moments before, while he was enjoying a sunny stroll along the water's edge, a slight misstep had sent him plunging over a rocky cliff and into the raging whirlpools below. Now, regaining some composure, he began to swim determinedly, fighting the sucking currents that drew him farther and farther from shore.

The scaled leviathan rose swiftly through the dark waters, a cruelly efficient, cold-blooded predator. It had sensed the presence of nearby prey: Rapid, rhythmic vibrations alerted the beast's primordial sensory organs. Excited, its rapacious appetite stimulated, it altered course slightly and sped up, closing in on the source. Time to kill.

ALASKA LEMMING

RECIPE

HOOK: TMC 8089, size 2-6

THREAD: Brown Flat Waxed Nylon

TAIL AND LEGS:
Large black round rubber

BACK: Coarse deer hair

BELLY: Brown Australian possum or similar fur, left on hide

HEAD: Dense foam popper/slider head (available from Edgewater Products)

EYES: 3-D plastic eyes, gold/black or to preference

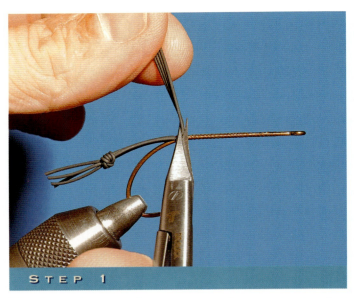

STEP 1

STEP 2

Wind a solid underbody of thread, ending near the bend of the hook. From a band of large, round black rubber strands, peel off three strands. Leave them connected—this makes them easier to work with. Tie an overhand knot a couple of inches from one end of the strands, drawing the knot tight. This is important: If the knot isn't drawn down snugly, it will come undone while fishing. Separate the shorter individual strands just past the knot. Lay the longer, connected strands on top of the hook shank, and wind firmly in place. Take care not to wrap too far forward (the deer hair will flare easier over less bulk). Snip the separated strands to a length of about an inch—this forms the end of the tail. Once the rubber is tied in, you needn't worry about the strands separating, as the knot ensures the tail assembly will retain its correct configuration.

To form the "back" of the lemming, you'll need to find some fairly long, hollow hair. I like deer body, but elk also works just fine. Be careful to choose hair that is somewhat coarse and has a lot of body. If the hair is too fine, it won't provide enough buoyancy; you'll need to tie in excessive amounts in order to achieve the desired bulky profile. Light-colored elk body hair is also nice as it shows up well on the water under almost any glare conditions, while dark hair disappears if thrown or drifted into shadow. First, prepare the hair, trimming it close to the hide, then combing or "flicking" out all of the underfur. Place the clumps, tips down, into a hair stacker. Tap the stacker on your tabletop several times. (For large bunches of hair like this, I find many moderate taps much more effective than a few very hard bangs, both to even the hair tips and to keep peace in your marriage.) Then turn it sideways and remove the short end, exposing the aligned hair tips. To form the high-silhouette back of the fly, you want to attach the hair clumps so they flare at an approximate 180-degree arc over the top of the hook. Achieve this by squeezing the clump to the top of the hook shank. Then bring the thread over the top of the hair and snug down on the far side of the shank. I use at least 3/0 thread as it has the power to really cinch down the hair. (Do not "spin" the hair on by winding two loose wraps around the hair and hook, then drawing it tight—this will give you a 360-degree flare, which is not desirable.) Wind a few more wraps of thread forward, to secure the hair in place. Clip off all the blunt butt ends of hair flush with the hook shank; the tips of the hair should reach to about the knot in your fly's tail.

Repeat the steps above to attach a second bunch of hair. When secured in place, the tips of this clump of stacked hair should be just shorter than those of the first. Again, wrap forward through the blunt ends to secure the hair in place, and then trim them off. Thread bulk isn't really much of a consideration on this pattern, so I'll usually take several more wraps to tie down any stray hairs.

Next, prepare the first two sets of legs for your lemming by repeating the steps used to form the tail. This should give you two separate appendages, both identical to the tail. Tie in the first leg on the near side of the hook, attaching it just forward of the hair, then wrapping back over the rubber until the leg is snug against the hair. The legs should be at a bit of an upward angle, actually lying along and sticking out to the side of the hair. To achieve this, simply elevate the angle of the leg as you wrap the thread back over it. This isn't critical—it's more a tying quirk of mine—but make sure the legs don't extend below the midway point of the hook axis.

The swimmer was gaining now, slowly but perceptibly closing the gap between himself and the shore. Although he was tiring, the worst was over—the nearer to the shallows he got, the weaker the water's dragging grasp became. Relaxing slightly, he settled into a steady cadence.

The monster had spotted its quarry. Now it closed in on the doggedly paddling form. With a final push of its mammoth tail, it hurtled forward, mouth gaping, ragged rows of teeth exposed, feeling the hapless creature succumb to its powerful suctioning inhalation. The swimmer sensed a sudden surge in the water beneath his churning legs, felt himself rise up on a wave, then slide inexplicably backwards, as if on a slippery slope, then . . .

The Alaska Lemming offers the best of all worlds: the buoyancy of foam and deer hair, the fur-belly "anchor" to prevent the fly from landing or flipping upside down, and wriggling rubber legs that twitch and tantalize.

Abruptly, the massive beast was thrown sideways and almost completely free of the water. Unimaginably, in its bloodlust, the great fish had not noticed the steeply angled shoreline until it was too late, and now thrashed about, high-centered on the shallow rocks. Disoriented, at once frantic to regain the safety of the depths and frustrated at the loss of its certain meal, the predator hesitated briefly before self-preservation overcame hunger, and it rooster-tailed purposefully back into the depths.

"Whoa!" I yelled to Jim. "*Did you see that?*"

"Did I see what?"

"A mouse fell into the water! It was trying to swim back to shore and it was almost there when all of a sudden this giant trout exploded out of the water behind it and practically flew up onto the bank trying to grab it. Then it was flopping around in the shallows. I don't know what happened to the mouse but I think it got away—geez, that fish was huge!"

Jim peered at me, apparently more than a little concerned at this verbal torrent: "A mouse?"

"Yeah. It was swimming—maybe it was a lemming, I don't know—and, geez, *did you see the size of that trout?*"

"Well, uh, no…I guess I missed it."

"It was huge!" Realizing I was repeating myself, I

STEP 5

Repeat the step with the second leg, on the far side of the hook. Trim the butt ends of the rubber legs.

STEP 7

Repeat Steps 4 and 5, to create the forward set of legs. Everything is the same here—remember to keep the legs tilted at a bit of an upward angle.

STEP 6

Prepare another clump of hair and tie it down immediately in front of the legs. Again, make the hair tips just short of the length of the previous bunch—this will continue the stacked "hedgehog" appearance of the fly. After clipping off the butt ends, repeat the step with another hair clump. Note how these hair bunches cover the lower parts of the legs, leaving just the feet extending. Actual lemming legs are quite short, so I find this profile works perfectly.

STEP 8

Repeat Step 6, tying in two more bunches of hair. Make sure each bunch ties in slightly shorter than the previous. Take several wraps to clean up any remaining fibers of hair.

STEP 9

Prepare the belly segment. I like to purchase complete skins (in this case Australian possum, though other dark-haired animals will work just fine), making sure the hide has been tanned to a soft, supple texture. If the hide is rigid, you'll find it very difficult to trim to shape; it won't want to conform to the hook properly. I find an X-Acto knife the best tool to make the cuts. Avoid scissors, as they tend to damage way too much of the fur. You'll want to lay the skin out, fur down, stretching it at all edges, if possible. Even a clipboard will help, although it allows attachment at only one end of the hide. With the skin at least somewhat taut, describe an "extended diamond" in it with the tip of the blade—a strip roughly the same length as the hair back of the fly, though the length of the fur will make the whole profile longer. You're shooting to have the belly fur extend back to about the length of the rubber tail. If possible, make the cut so that the direction of the fur (the way it lays down naturally) follows the length of your "skinny diamond." As long as the blade is new and sharp, this carving should be relatively effortless. Brush away any loose fur hanging off the edge of the hide. Removing the hook from the vise, lay the fur strip beneath it, so that the fur "lies down" pointing towards the hook eye. Impale the hide with the hook point at a spot a short distance from the tip of and in the center of the diamond. Slide the fur strip up until it snugs against the tail tie-in and can slide no farther.

stopped gibbering, took a deep breath, and reached with shaking fingers for my fly box.

Gaining dry ground at last, the swimmer lay gasping for several long moments, then pulled himself to his feet and crept cautiously back through the tall grass toward home.

* * * * * * *

This happened nearly 20 years ago on a small creek deep within the Togiak Wilderness Area of western Alaska. It was the first time I had seen a trout try to inhale a waterborne lemming. The impression the episode left was indelible. It was brutal, visceral, exhilarating to watch. And it opened my eyes to a whole new realm of fishing: skating mouse patterns for carnivorous trout.

The stream, I now realize, was practically custom-designed for mousing. Shallow and braided, each tiny side channel was choked with downed spruce and alder trees. Banks were hung over with draping grasses. Better yet, every 50 feet or so the miniature, meandering creek twisted at a 90-degree angle, gouging deep, inviting potholes in the gravelly streambed. In fact, before we had departed camp on this, our first day in the bush, the lodge's owner had gathered us by the jet boats, proclaiming the lemmings to be at the peak of their seven-year life cycle. If we had brought any mouse patterns, we should give serious thought to using them. Kind of a smoke-'em-if-you-got-'em brand of pep talk. We all nodded politely, and then went back to knotting egg patterns to our leaders—we were here to catch fish, not be led off on some piscatorial snipe hunt.

> **It was the first time I had seen a trout try to inhale a waterborne lemming. The impression the episode left was indelible. It was brutal, visceral, exhilarating to watch.**

I've never been able to verify the breeding statistics we were fed that morning, but I was soon to experience firsthand the fecundity of the furry little critters. They were everywhere: scurrying underfoot in the tall, riverside beargrass; floating dead, en masse, like so many miniature bloated cows in backwater eddies; they even showed up—horribly enough—on the boardwalk beneath my bare toes on moonless nocturnal treks to the outhouse.

Much to our surprise that first day, nearly everyone in our group reported watching fat rainbows casually waking to the surface and slurping down these struggling rodents. Before long, everyone was pitching mouse patterns by day and spinning deer hair by lantern light each night.

To this day, I've never seen a more prolific "hatch" of these little mammals. What I've discovered in the ensuing years, however, is that imitations of them will often bring trophy trout to the surface, even where mice seem

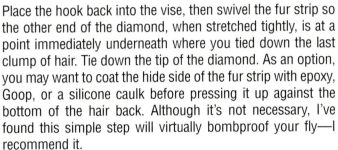

STEP 10

STEP 11

Place the hook back into the vise, then swivel the fur strip so the other end of the diamond, when stretched tightly, is at a point immediately underneath where you tied down the last clump of hair. Tie down the tip of the diamond. As an option, you may want to coat the hide side of the fur strip with epoxy, Goop, or a silicone caulk before pressing it up against the bottom of the hair back. Although it's not necessary, I've found this simple step will virtually bombproof your fly—I recommend it.

You're now ready to prepare and attach the foam head. I buy pre-formed popper/slider foam blanks from a fly shop— they're manufactured by Edgewater Fly Company. To get the right size, I buy the large ones, and then slice off the smaller end of the blank. Because the blanks tend to come in bright colors, I simply color the "heads" with a dark brown waterproof marking pen. If you can find brown blanks to start with, more power to you! I'm not convinced trout care what color they are, though. I suggest sizing the head with a trial-run fitting; make sure you can push the head on over the hook eye and back far enough on the shank so that the hook eye just clears the front of the foam head. Note that there is a slight taper to the head—the smaller end should be to the front of the fly. Pull the head off and apply a dollop of 5 Minute Epoxy to the thread wraps covering the front part of the hook, being careful not to get any in the eye of the hook.

STEP 12

Press the head back onto the hook. If necessary, hold it in place for a few minutes until the epoxy sets up—this will prevent the head from creeping forward and obscuring the hook eye. Within 20 minutes, it will be immovable.

STEP 13

Some 3-D eyes come with plastic pegs attached to their backs; if so, clip the pegs off flush to the back of the eye (a pair of heavy-duty nippers from your local hardware store will keep you from ruining your scissors). If you can find the eyes sans pegs, all the better. Feel free to experiment with different styles of eyes to suit your taste. Dab a bit of the 5 Minute Epoxy to the back of the eye and press it onto the head until the epoxy sets up, repeating the process on the far side of the fly. Go fish!

absent. When I'm exploring new waters in Alaska or Russia, a lemming pattern is often my searching pattern of choice, both for its effectiveness and for the always-memorable takes. At one time mouse flies were thought to be effective only during early or late season, when no salmon were present in the rivers. I've found mousing excellent throughout the season. I've even pulled up trout over active sockeye spawning beds. Skating these oversized surface patterns may be one of the last over-looked techniques for trout in our 49th state.

Despite the wonderful memories I have of fishing lemmings, for many years I was frustrated by the lackluster performance of the available patterns. In a word, they sunk. No matter how tightly the hair was packed, regard-less of how often floatant was applied, none of them would continue skating for more than five or six fish. After that they would become waterlogged and useless. Like others, for years I simply carried a bunch of these standard patterns with me, so I could switch flies when maximum saturation level was reached. But this seemed an inefficient strategy. I needed to create a fly that would float for a long time. I also wanted a pattern that looked right—in both profile and movement.

> **As always, my innovation began with the hook. I needed a hook large enough to allow adequate hooking gape, considering the bulky mass essential to the pattern, with a wire diameter thin enough to allow easy penetration.**

As always, my innovation began with the hook. I needed a hook large enough to allow adequate hooking gape, considering the bulky mass essential to the pattern, with a wire diameter thin enough to allow easy penetration. At the time, a common problem with lemming patterns was the use of heavy, long-shank streamer hooks. The gapes of these models were woefully inadequate; the often-heavy irons were too thick for solid hook-ups. With these two strikes already against you, the hooked-to-landed ratio was abysmal.

After much experimentation, I opted for a stinger-style hook, a model designed and used for bass poppers (which is essentially what I was tying, but for trout). The most noticeable feature of this hook is the elongated bend of the shank, resulting in a very large gape—perfect for what I had in mind. Also, the wire was thin, and its history with bass assured me of its strength and resistance to bending open.

Interestingly, over the years I've met with dissent over my use of this style of hook: "It kills fish!" Though I understand and appreciate the sentiment completely, it simply isn't true. Allow me to explain why.

When fishing Lemmings, fishers kill fish, not hooks—more to the point, the techniques employed by fishers kill fish. When a fish eats a mouse, it does so with aggression and authority. Without trying to attribute human characteristics to trout, I suspect they do so to get it down quickly, to minimize resistance from the prey. Regardless of the ferocity of the hit (and there is considerable variation), it's obvious that, as with my dogs and any food scraps smaller than their heads, the object is to get the food to the gullet immediately. To accomplish this, fish tend to employ an inhale-and-gulp style of take.

If the Lemming pattern is presented on a dead drift, with no tension on the line, the trout will have a hook deep in the gills or throat in a heartbeat, likely resulting in injury or death.

The key is to always skate the fly on a tight line, which better emulates the movement of a swimming mouse anyway. Then, when a trout grabs, it will nearly always be hooked in the mouth; the tension on the line makes it difficult for it to swallow the fly. To further reduce gill damage, try tying the pattern inverted, with the point of the hook facing up.

these two styles of flies over the years have proved this rule to be true beyond a shadow of a doubt in my mind.

The next decision was a bit less critical: What to use for a tail?

Though you'll often see long, rat-like appendages protruding from the back of conventional mouse patterns, actual lemmings and voles have surprisingly short tails. I wanted this feature to be realistic in length yet have a good amount of motion in the water and be durable. I tried many materials, including ribbons of leather, wide rubber bands, marabou, and rabbit strips. Most of these tended to be too soft when wet, fouling around the hook

> **Regardless of the ferocity of the hit (and there is considerable variation), it's obvious that, as with my dogs and any food scraps smaller than their heads, the object is to get the food to the gullet immediately.**

An articulated version of the Alaska Lemming. Its sinuous movement across the water's surface provokes mind-blowing assaults from carnivorous wild trout.

It's worth mentioning that this same rule can apply to large-hooked subsurface patterns as well. A perfect example is the meaty, articulated "flesh fly" patterns commonly used in Alaska and Russia to imitate drifting chunks of rotten salmon carcass. They're four to six inches long with a trailing hook. If no tension is kept on the line while drifting such a monster fly through a run, trout will engulf it aggressively, many becoming gill-hooked. If the same fly is fished on a tight-line swing, the problem is significantly minimalized. The thousands of trout I've hooked with

an annoying percentage of the time.

The rubber bands were the best, which gave me the idea of using strands of round rubber, knotted near the ends. These provided the proper stiffness, were active when pulled through the water, and fish couldn't chew them off, no matter how hard they tried. I decided then and there that I had also discovered the perfect material to make Lemming legs, and was indeed very happy with the back-and-forth swimming motions these rubber bundles made while I dragged the fly across the water's surface.

What I would use for the top of my Lemming was never in question. Deer hair is buoyant, can be spun to shape and has a high profile, making it easy to see on the water. Because I wanted this buoyancy only on the dorsal portion of the fly, I flared my stacked clumps exclusively on the top half, being careful to keep the aligned hair tips at approximately the same height.

From experience, I knew what I needed from the belly of my fly: an anchor point—not overpowering the buoyancy of the pattern, but achieving the realistic "sinking butt" profile of the natural. Also, if designed correctly, this feature would serve to eliminate the maddening tendency that some clipped-hair mouse patterns have of flipping upside down upon landing. Sometimes mousing is

Thus began my search for the perfect belly hair. I knew I wanted to use fur still on the hide, as it could be stretched to best imitate the creature's fuzzy underside. After mole hair, my first choice, was a flop (it looked fantastic, absolutely real when wet, but didn't soak up enough water and allowed the fly to turtle over from time to time), I decided to try longer-fibered hairs. Rabbit worked, and is still a good choice, as are beaver and muskrat. I prefer them all dyed brown, though the fish don't seem to care.

From experience, I knew what I needed from the belly of my fly: an anchor point— not overpowering the buoyancy of the pattern, but achieving the realistic "sinking butt" profile of the natural.

a one-shot deal. If your first cast over a fish is ruined by an ass-over-teakettle presentation, the game is over.

My first thought was to simply tie lead strips to the bottom of the hook shank. While this would have served to accomplish my goal, it seemed somehow counterproductive for a fly that had to float. It would also do nothing to effect my second goal, which was to show the fish something that really looked like a lemming's belly. This is, after all, mostly what the fish sees of a swimming rodent. So, I reasoned, why not use the real thing—why not fur?

When I happened on Australian possum, I knew I had my perfect match. It kept its bulk when wet, sucked up enough water to assure the fly would be belly-heavy and land correctly, and had a superb, fleshy look. Dyed a dark brown, it was exactly what I wanted. Attaching it is easy: Simply trim a diamond-shaped portion from the hide (the pelt needs to be tanned to a malleable softness) and thread the hook through the hide near one pointed end. Slide the hide up the hook bend, snugging it against the tail tie-in area. Stretch the other pointed end forward tightly, coat the bare hide with a thin layer of Goop or 5

Minute Epoxy, and tie it down approximately where the deer hair ends, pressing the hide against the underside of the deer-hair tie-ins.

When introduced (nearly always unwillingly!) to water, lemmings swim much like dogs: head up, butt down, legs paddling furiously. For the final step of my pattern, I needed a "head" that would allow the fly to be dragged across the surface of the water repeatedly without becoming waterlogged. Believe it or not, my first attempts were with wood! After the balsa heads were destroyed in

these materials—was the perfect source for obtaining a ready-made mouse head. I took one of their larger slider-popper blanks, chopped it to the correct length, and used a brown waterproof marker to color it. I added a couple of bulging eyes for looks, epoxied the whole unit in place, and I had a most practical and durable Lemming.

I designed my Alaskan Lemming for function. The pattern has undergone the ultimate test during the last two years, as hundreds went to the Russian Kamchatka to be used on tens of thousands of the region's broad-shouldered

Sometimes mousing is a one-shot deal. If your first cast over a fish is ruined by an ass-over-teakettle presentation, the game is over.

short order and various hardwoods proved to be marginal floaters that were arduous to construct, it finally occurred to me to try foam. Not only is foam more buoyant than wood, I reasoned, but the fish would be less likely to instantly reject the softer texture. What wasn't immediately obvious, however, was the best type of foam to use.

After much experimentation, I came to realize a dense closed-cell foam was preferable to an open-cell style, as the latter quickly absorbs water when asked to support significant weight. Edgewater Fishing Products, makers of an infinite variety of foam cones, cylinders and blocks—and their own line of creative flies incorporating

rainbows. These virgin trout eat mice like nowhere else on Earth, making a skated facsimile the angler's most popular approach. My greatest compliment came when the pattern got a resounding stamp of approval from guides and clients alike, each of whom came to refer to it as their "lemming of choice."

Two new twists were added by ingenious guides and are worth mentioning.

First, even this pattern will eventually succumb to the problem of sinking. When it did, guide Mike VanWormer started wrapping a simple riffling hitch behind the foam head. Presto—you've just added another couple of hours to the fly's floating life! Second, some of the guides used a razor blade to shave the bottom of the foam head at an angle, starting at the hook eye and working down and away from the hook's shank. This forces the fly to plane upwards when skated in heavy water, a cool little trick.

There are a number of ways to fool these fish, but for sheer visual drama, nothing comes close to that moment when predator becomes prey, when a confident, leopard-spotted rainbow crushes your giant dry fly right off the water's surface.

Many imitations of this miniature swimming pork roast will catch fish, but few incorporate all the unique and useful features found in this fly. Rest assured that Arctic trout see these critters—lemmings, voles, mice, whatever you want to call them—as lunch. I also tie a longer-bodied, articulated version of the Lemming, which undulates seductively when skated. It also more accurately represents the actual size of the naturals. Frankly, the only real reason to use it is the ferocity of the strikes it evokes. Sometimes that's enough. After all, there are a number of ways to fool these fish, but for sheer visual drama, nothing comes close to that moment when predator becomes prey, when a confident, leopard-spotted rainbow crushes your giant dry fly right off the water's surface.

PMD Trigger Nymph

"WHAT IN THE HECK…" I muttered under my breath, scrutinizing the long, amber shadow with growing frustration. I'd felt pretty good about spotting him in the tiny spring creek in the first place, tucked up under the overhanging grasses the way he was. A five-minute stalk on hands and knees later, I had peeked my head up slowly, just in time to see him drift out from the bank and intercept another subsurface meal.

"You're mine," I gloated. Half an hour later, my tortured, aching knees told me to get up and go find another fish, but my pride just wouldn't allow it. The 20-inch brown continued feeding with maddening regularity in ankle-deep water—a bank feeder no less, my absolute favorite—unaware of my presence, despite scores of presentations.

PMD TRIGGER NYMPH

RECIPE

HOOK:	TMC 3761, size 14-18
THREAD:	Camel UNI 8/0
TAIL:	Ringneck pheasant tail fibers
ABDOMEN	Rusty-brown turkey biot
THORAX:	Mercer's Select Buggy Nymph Dubbing, Trigger Nymph Brown
EXPLODING WINGS:	
	Pale-yellow Ice Dub or equivalent
LEGS:	Mottled-brown partridge hackle fibers
COLLAR:	Same as thorax
BEAD:	Gold metal bead to match size of hook

STEP 1

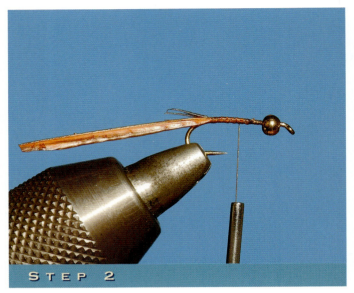

STEP 2

Slide a small gold bead on the hook all the way to the eye. Copper is another effective color. (Although I've experimented with glass bead heads, I've had surprisingly little success with them on this pattern.) Form a sparse base with your thread from the bead back to a point directly in front of the bend of the hook. Select three fibers from the copperish-brown side of a ringneck pheasant tail feather, taken from the center of the entire tail splay. It's important to use these fibers, as the softer tan fibers found on the outside feathers typically won't separate and splay correctly. Use your fingers to make sure the fiber tips are aligned evenly, then pinch them to the top of the hook at a point just forward of the bend; tie them down. If there is thread in back of the feather tie-down spot, wrap the thread back over the fibers until you reach that original tie-down, while gently pulling the fibers back and upward. When you release the fibers, they should splay apart from each other slightly. If not, simply push them up from underneath with your thumbnail or the side of a scissor blade—this will accomplish the desired look. If you've ever watched a natural mayfly nymph resting in the water column between bursts of swimming, you've noticed how frequently it raises and splays its tails, presumably to keep from sinking back down. Wrap the fibers down to a point just behind the bead and trim off the excess.

Trim a single biot from the feather stem. If you look at the cut section of the biot from the perspective of the trimmed end, you'll see that the feather has a concave configuration running down its entire length. To achieve the desired "ridged-edge" segmented effect, you need to tie in the pointed end of the biot just behind the bead. Working back, make sure that both edges of the biot curve away from you. Imagine the biot is a drinking straw that's been cut in half lengthwise—you tie it in so the cut edges face away from you, and the rounded side toward you. Wrap back over the biot to the spot where you tied in the tail, then forward.

STEP 3

Coat the underbody of the abdomen with a thin layer of Flexament, then use your hackle pliers to grasp the loose end of the biot. (I recommend the J. Dorin brand pliers, as they grasp the feather firmly without slipping or breaking the biot, and they have fine, easily maneuverable tips.) Wrap the biot forward, evenly spacing each turn to achieve a realistic, naturally segmented silhouette. The wrapped biot should take up about two-thirds of the available hook shank. If the ridged edges don't pop up as you wrap the biot forward, it means you've tied in the feather backward. No worries—simply unwrap the thread, flip over the biot and tie it down again.

STEP 4

Tie off the biot and clip the excess feather. It's worth mentioning that this pattern also works pretty well if you tie in the biot "backward," which gives the abdomen a smooth, somewhat glossy finish. I prefer the distinctly segmented look, but you should experiment and draw your own conclusions. Cover the biot tie-down area with a short ball of dubbing. Don't twist on too much dubbing! The whole thorax should be pretty narrow, just slightly larger in diameter than the biot abdomen. Remember, real pale morning dun (*Ephemerella inermis*) nymphs are svelte; they're not big, chunky insects.

STEP 5

Choose a brown-speckled breast feather from a Hungarian partridge skin. If you use partridge as much as I do, do yourself a favor and buy a full skin. It'll give you many more feathers than a comparable dollar's worth of packaged feathers, and they'll be better quality. Pull off a few fibers from the stem of the feather, so the tips are fairly well aligned, and lash them to the far side of the hook. The tips should extend back to about the end of the biot abdomen. Repeat the process on the near side.

The worst thing was that I knew exactly what he was eating; the pale morning duns in this little Montana stream came off like clockwork at high noon every day in August. It was now 11 a.m. No rocket science here. The problem was, I'd shown the fish every small mayfly nymph in my box. The big trout rushed, sidled up to, drifted back with, and inspected most with split-second interest before turning away. My other flies he ignored outright. He was a player, and he was playing me. Grudgingly, I broke my concentration from the feeding brown, easing my tingling, circulation-starved legs out in front of me. I sat back against a grassy hummock to reassess the situation.

The sparse profile of the Trigger Nymph series lends itself well to *Callibaetis* variations. Tip: Understate the Ice Dub.

As if awakening from a dream, I became suddenly aware of the shroud of whining insects cocooning my head, the vision-impairing drops of sweat coursing down the curvature of my eyeglasses, and a decidedly unpleasant memory of the morning's gas-station breakfast coming back to life in my stomach.

Focus, I lectured myself. Poking through my flies, I pondered my options. More nymphs.... Why torture myself? A streamer might do the trick, but I knew it would be a one-shot deal and, with the sun high and brassy, I didn't like the odds. Dries? I was pretty sure the object of my desire would be happily slurping pretty little olive sailboats in about an hour, but waiting for that was out of the question. This fish was feeding steadily—if I couldn't solve the puzzle now, fishing for him on the surface would be anticlimactic, and more than a little demoralizing.

So what to try? Just as my overtaxed brain began to short out, I saw it: Tucked into a corner of my fly box, hidden beneath a cluster of Prince Nymphs, was a perfect little PMD floating nymph.

I'm not exactly sure what drew me to it. After all, it was a dry fly, designed for that moment when emerging mayflies hang suspended in the film, vigorously squirming their way to flight. The pattern was a predecessor to many of the partially submerged emergers we see today. But my fish was not showing the slightest inclination to look up.

Nonetheless, in one of those strange, "ah-ha" moments that sometimes seem to arrive uninvited, I

STEP 6

Dub a bit more of the thorax, stopping at a point just short of the bead. Wrap the last turn of dubbed thread back toward the tail of the fly so that, when you run out of dubbing, the thread is just about dead center in the middle of the dubbed thorax.

STEP 8

If you've ever tied a floating nymph "ball," this step is exactly the same. Swing around the dubbed thread so it points directly up, at a right angle to the hook shank. Keeping tension on the thread with your bobbin hand, run your other thumb and forefinger down the thread, squashing the Ice Dub into a ball that perches on the top of the brown-dubbed thorax. Immediately pull down the thread on the far side of the thorax, while continuing to squeeze the Ice Dub ball in place on top of the thorax. One more revolution of the thread around the hook shank at this point will lock the ball in place.

STEP 7

Dub a thin "noodle" of the Ice Dub, leaving a short gap of bare thread between it and the hook shank. A little of this stuff goes a long way, so keep it sparse—overdo it and you may scare as many fish as you attract.

STEP 9

Dub a little more of the thread with the brown blend. Wind a wrap of this sparse dubbing both behind and in front of the wing bud—this defines the position of the bright ball as being on top of the thorax, and covers up any bare hook shank left adjacent to the bead. Tie off the thread.

The finished PMD Trigger nymph.

pulled out the fly, knotted it to my 6X tippet beneath a tiny micro-shot, and flipped it above the trout.

My cast wasn't particularly good. So when the fish casually moved three feet off the bank and inhaled my first presentation, I was shocked, and completely farmed the strike. Amazingly, the big brown didn't spook. He seemed merely surprised, still searching for his lost appetizer. Another cast and he shot forward, confidently engulfing the fly again. This time I was ready. I struck quickly and firmly—once again the diminutive bug scraped out of its mouth.

Incredibly, this really got the fish's attention. I watched astonished as it darted back and forth, frantically hunting for its elusive meal. Another cast, another missed strike—*this couldn't be happening!* I was now beside myself, mainlining on adrenaline and bewilderment. With trembling fingers I plucked the fly from the air to take a look.

Vary the colors of tail, abdomen, thorax and Ice Dub wings to create your own versions of the Trigger Nymph.

"Oh, no," I groaned. The hook had broken at the shank, no doubt on the first grab, when my too-late over-reaction had apparently actually sunk home. Close inspection showed a spot of rust at the point of failure—operator error.

Looking up, I noticed a palpable change in the trout's behavior—no longer confident in its mannerisms, it had returned to the bank, and hung there nervously. There would be no more chances for him this day. Besides, that had been my one and only "floating" nymph.

I went on to have one of those memorable summer afternoons, enjoying nearly four hours of rising trout, flushed snipe, furry meadow voles glimpsed scurrying underfoot through the tall grass, and a big whitetail doe I nearly tripped over skirting a flooded backwater. As I trudged back to my truck at day's end, my mind drifted back to that big brown. Why had it refused my nymphs, yet jumped so eagerly on the sunken dry? The tails of both were essentially the same. Both patterns had ribbed body configurations. And they sprouted nearly identical partridge legs. The nymphs all had dark wing cases and the floating nymph had a pale-yellowish pad.

Ha! Choosing the pattern earlier had been blind luck, but now a worm of understanding began wriggling in my mind. While I've always considered the choice of wing-pad color on floating nymphs a moot point (after all, this feature is designed be above the water, on top of the fly, out of the fish's vision), in this case the trout was able to see it. It's a safe bet fish don't observe colors the same way we do, but I was sure there was significance in the light-colored wing case.

a third of them had already begun the process of emerging, well beneath the surface of the water. Some merely had split wing cases, while others had heads and parts of their wings showing, but they all had one thing in common: The visible part of the emerging adult insect was much brighter and lighter in color than the surrounding shuck.

I was now certain my bank-feeding friend had been

Just as my overtaxed brain began to short out, I saw it: Tucked into a corner of my fly box, hidden beneath a cluster of Prince nymphs, was a perfect little PMD floating nymph.

The next morning at 11:15, I was at the same place with my nemesis nowhere in sight, which made my job easier. Easing into the gentle flow, I submerged a fine-meshed seine, holding it just above sinuously flowing weeds in the clear, icy flow until my hands felt like numb stumps. Stumbling back to shore, I laid the netting on a bed of clover and investigated my catch. Scuds dominated the collection, with liberal doses of aquatic worms and little crawling things far too tiny to identify. Nothing very enlightening here.

Fifteen minutes later, without much enthusiasm, and badly wanting to string up a rod, I waded back out for another sampling. Paydirt! This time the mesh was alive with thrashing mayfly nymphs. As I had suspected, nearly

feeding selectively on these partially emerged specimens. While the obvious thing would have been to tie more of the same floating nymphs that had fooled him, I believed the pattern could be improved to match the situation.

Some new fly-tying materials speak to me the first time I see them at a fly shop, almost jumping off the shelf with possibility. Others niggle away at the back of my consciousness, ideas for their use slowly crawling toward the light of epiphany. The latter was the case with Ice Dub, an intriguing holographic dubbing introduced by Hareline Dubbin. The moment I held the mix up to a light, I was captivated by its translucent, light-refracting qualities and wide range of colors. Of particular importance, it was fine enough to dub even small flies. Its flash

A Trigger Caddis, one of many offshoots possible with this style of tying, seems to fish best with a tungsten bead.

proved to be a bit overpowering if used to create entire bug bodies, though, so after a little more experimenting, I went on to other things, largely forgetting about the material.

That very moment in Montana when I realized I wanted to create a sinking version of the floating nymph pattern, Ice Dub jumped immediately back to mind. I was sure it would be the perfect choice for the light-colored sphere on top of the nymph's thorax, accurately emulating the contrast between shuck and emerging insect, the latter bright with natural color.

Modify color and body configuration to create different patterns such as this Green Drake Trigger Nymph.

While the main trigger for the pattern would be the flashy dubbing ball, I imagined a number of other ways to create the overall illusion I desired.

First, splaying a trio of reddish brown pheasant-tail fibers would mimic the three slightly hairy tails of the natural. To give my fly the subtle abdominal segmentation Nature gave its living counterpart, I used a turkey biot, tied so that tiny ridges appeared with each wrap of the feather. Anyone who has observed the full-body whiplash efforts of an emerging mayfly remembers all the motion involved—whether the bugs actually use their legs to propel themselves or not, I figured including them on my pattern would add enticing movement. That was a no-brainer. Plus, partridge fibers display a speckled look that is as close to aquatic-insect mottling as anything I know, and their use inspires my confidence. Finally, a bit of thorax dubbing to match the abdomen color, and a metal bead

head (you'll have to trust me here; the pattern fishes better with the bead), and the pattern was complete.

Yes, the nymph was successful, enough so to inspire the creation of many variations on the theme. I've incorporated different materials to best match varying insect characteristics, and always use the Ice Dub on top. This approach is more formulaic than specific—a tying style rather than a pattern, really—and can easily be adapted to any tier's personal preferences.

The gluttonous tendencies of trout are exposed when they see the "emerging wings" of this Hex Trigger Nymph.

Like many nymphs, those in the Trigger series seem to fish better as they get roughed up with the catching of a few fish. Noticeably, the dubbing ball will begin to lose its form as this occurs, causing stray fibers to stream back over the body. While at first dismaying, this phenomenon, I have come to realize, does not diminish the effectiveness of the fly, and in fact sometimes enhances it, perhaps by emulating the swept-back profile of the wings of drowned insects. If so, it's just more blind luck, but I'll take it.

Though designed as a generic dark nymph, I'm confident the Peacock Trigger Nymph is taken as an emerging *Isonychia* mayfly by many fish.

GOLD BEAD BIOT EPOXY GOLDEN STONE NYMPH

I HAVE A LONG AND I'M AFRAID SOMEWHAT CHECKERED HISTORY with stonefly nymphs. Somewhere around my 10th year, a neighbor, tiring of my hangdog look and perpetual habitation of his living room jabbering incessantly about the latest "Early Season Trouting" article I'd read, invited me to join him and his sons on their annual opening-day camping trip. Though little memory remains of that grand adventure, I do recall vividly his obvious scorn for all the "tourists" perched on the banks drowning salmon eggs.

"Let me show you a little secret," he winked, slipping his hand beneath the water and pulling up a large, shiny rock. "See 'em?" he asked, pointing to all the aquatic insects scurrying wildly about their suddenly altered universe. "Those little periwinkles are what the trout really eat." Plucking off the largest, most dangerous-looking bugs, he carefully replaced the stone, and shoved the captured monsters into a small bait tin on his belt.

GOLD BEAD BIOT EPOXY GOLDEN STONE NYMPH

RECIPE

HOOK: TMC 2302, size 6-12

THREAD: Tan UNI 8/0

TAIL AND ANTENNAE:
Sulfur-orange turkey biots, mottled with brown marking pen

ABDOMEN Sulfur-orange turkey biots, mottled with brown marking pen

THORAX: Mercer's Select Buggy Nymph Dubbing, Golden Stone

WING CASE: Mottled, dark golden-brown turkey tail

WING CASE GLOSS:
Devcon 5 Minute Epoxy

LEGS: Mottled brown hen-back feather

COLLAR: Same as thorax, marked on dorsal side only with brown marking pen

BEAD: Gold metal bead to match size of hook

STEP 1

Slip the bead onto the hook shank. Select two matching turkey biots, from the top of the main feather—the narrower the biots, the better. Lay one on each side of the hook shank, so the natural curvature of the biots flares them away from each other. If you have trouble attaining a noticeable spread, try dubbing a tiny ball right where the tails will be attached. When you tie in the biots and wrap back over them to the dubbing ball, it will force them to flare.

STEP 2

Cut two segments of the non-toxic wire, each approximately twice the length of the hook shank. (I find starting with longer strips makes the wire easier to work with, as opposed to attempting to cut the perfect lengths initially.) Cut one end of each strip at an angle. Lash one strip onto the near side of the hook shank, with the beveled end terminating at a point just short of the hook bend, right where the tails are tied in.

STEP 3

Repeat the process on the far side of the hook shank. When both wires are attached, clip them at a point approximately two-thirds of the way up the hook shank. Lock the wires into place. Form a smooth, tapered underbody with additional wraps of the tying thread.

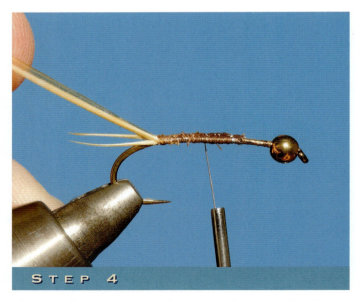

STEP 4

Tie in a turkey biot for the abdomen, being careful to choose one of the longest from the main feather. Attach it by its tip, so that the concave side of the feather faces away from you—this will achieve the desired "segmented" effect as you wrap it forward. (If you don't see pronounced ridges as you wind on the biot, you'll know it was tied in backwards.) Before actually wrapping the biot forward, spread a coat of Flexament onto the underbody—this will add tremendous durability to the finished fly.

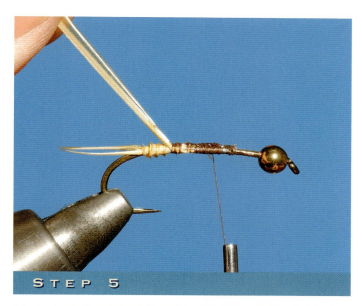

STEP 5

If you haven't reached the midpoint of the hook shank after winding one biot, tie in another and repeat the process.

STEP 6

Whip-finish the thread immediately in front of the abdomen, slip the bead back as far as it will go, and re-attach the thread behind the eye of the hook. Essentially, repeat the steps used for the tail to create the antennae, though they should only be about two-thirds the length.

Hardened worm-fishing veteran that I already was, even I flinched slightly watching him impale one of the nasty, thrashing little beasts on a hook. "You ever get bit?" I asked nervously.

"No," he laughed, "they look bad, but they don't bite." The creek was tiny, not more than a long hop across, but deep. In most places, long, draping grasses made indistinct the demarcation between shore and water, so we approached cautiously. Keeping a low profile, my tutor swung his rod back, then forward, pendulum-like, dropping the bait with a soft splat against the far bank. I watched as the weight of the bug pulled line under, and envisioned what might be lurking below.

Suddenly, the line slowed, stuttered, and appeared to cut upstream. With a quick wrist-flip, he set the hook and an unseen creature pulled doggedly against the lift of the rod. Gently, my neighbor slid the flopping trout from the water; I watched as it effortlessly found his hand.

Streams across the country are loaded with small, light-colored stonefly nymphs. Downsize the G. B. Biot Epoxy Golden Stone for a perfect imitation. Tie some with tungsten beads.

I flinched slightly watching him impale one of the nasty, thrashing little beasts on a hook. "You ever get bit?" I asked nervously. "No," he laughed, "they look bad, but they don't bite."

"Here," he offered, "take a look." Crowding close, I gazed at the bejeweled slip of a fish, captivated by its peppered palette of crimson and black sides, dark-green vermiculated back, and snowy-tipped fins. It was a brookie, I knew—the first I'd ever seen.

"Look for the biggest rocks," my neighbor instructed. "That's where the periwinkles like it best. Especially those black volcanic ones." With this sage piece of advice imparted, he moved off upstream, eager to be free of the gawking campers.

He knew what he was talking about. Within minutes the front pocket of my well-worn canvas satchel was seething with scrabbling brown and yellow creatures, and proud thoughts of a bulging creel filled my head. Indeed,

STEP 7

Clip off the butt ends of the biots. Tie off the thread again, slip the bead over the top of the antenna tie-down, and re-attach the thread in the thorax area.

STEP 9

Form a thread loop immediately in front of the abdomen, inserting a dubbing twister and sparse clumps of dubbing into it. Bring your thread forward to a point just behind the bead.

STEP 8

Tie in two strips of turkey tail for the wing case, one directly on top of the other. Wrap over the feathers until they are flush with the front of the abdomen, and directly on top of the hook shank.

STEP 10

Using the dubbing twister, spin the thread loop, forming a furry "rope" of dubbing.

S T E P   1 1

Wind the rope forward evenly, tying it off a short distance behind the bead—clip and discard the unused portion.

S T E P   1 2

Using a dubbing teaser, pick out heavy amounts of the dubbing to the sides of the thorax, creating a wide, flattened silhouette. Clip *the top only* of the dubbed thorax flush with the top of the hook shank.

a full limit of trout is exactly what I returned to camp with a short time later, including a few trophies approaching the magical 12-inch mark. Though I didn't realize it at the time, I had just begun my lifelong fascination with stoneflies.

I'm happy to say I learned the pleasures of catch-and-release angling a few short seasons later. Had I not, I'm confident I would have continued to wreak the irrevocable damage of a mobile copper mine, stripping local streams of all fish life, so effective was the technique I'd learned that day. Eventually, though, the method became a bit boring, its payoff a little too predictable. At about that same time, I began my odyssey into fly fishing. Devouring a prized copy of Ernest Schwiebert's *Nymphs*, I first learned the identities of the aquatic insects that had afforded me so much success. The author's exquisite illustrations of *Acroneuria californica* captured my attention; his tying recipes fired my imagination. Imitating the golden stonefly nymph became a passion.

> **For years, rudimentary yarn-bodied patterns were my standbys. I then struggled with dubbed-body patterns for quite a while, finally coming up with some unique flies that worked, but still didn't have that magic look I desired.**

For years, rudimentary yarn-bodied patterns were my standbys. I used wool or burlap strands that accurately matched the amber ventral coloration of the naturals, dark turkey-tail wing cases, and grouse hackles for legs. Trout liked them and they were easy to tie, but to my eye they left room for a lot of improvement. I then struggled with dubbed-body patterns for quite a while, finally coming up with some unique flies that worked, but still didn't have that magic look I desired.

The first time I saw one of Oliver Edwards's realistic golden stonefly nymphs, I just sat and stared, slack-jawed, a slight trickle of drool escaping my lips. *It looks better than the real thing,* I remember thinking. The only problem was, tying the pattern required the dexterity of a surgeon, and the patience of a monk, neither of which virtue is mine. Oliver's nymph inspired me, though, and I spent the next few days collecting and scrutinizing actual goldens in my local streams, something I'd never bothered with previously.

What I discovered was enlightening. Whereas I'd always thought of golden stone nymphs as being just smaller, lighter-colored versions of their aquatic roommate, the salmonfly, closer examination showed goldens possess a much flatter body profile. Also, though their bellies are indeed a rich golden hue, their dorsal colorations vary tremendously, often being very dark, apparently an adaptation designed to camouflage these

STEP 13

STEP 15

Pull or snip off the rounded tip of your "legs" feather, leaving a V-notch. Lay the feather flat on top of the thorax, with the notch pointing toward the rear of the fly. The point of the V should be just short of the end of the thorax. Strip the fibers from the feather's stem at its butt end, so that there are barbs protruding to the sides of the hook beginning just behind the bead (where the feather is tied in, as well). Clip off the remaining feather stem.

Repeat with the second strip, then trim the excess.

STEP 14

STEP 16

Pull the first wing case forward over the thorax, tying it down directly behind the bead. Don't stretch it too tightly, or the turkey strip will break into its individual fibers—not desirable, as it will allow the epoxy to seep through.

Using a fine-tipped bodkin or needle, apply a thin coat of 5 Minute Epoxy to the wing case. Don't concern yourself with the thickness of the epoxy at this point—simply make sure you cover every bit of the feather. As soon as this is accomplished, and before the epoxy starts to harden, place another drop of the epoxy in the middle of the wing case; it will immediately self-level, giving you a beautiful, glossy effect. The size of this second drop will determine how thick or "high" the finished wing case will be.

STEP 17

As soon as the epoxy is fully hardened, dub a short collar between the wing case and bead.

STEP 18

Using a waterproof brown marking pen, color the top of this collar and the back of the biot abdomen, as well as speckling the tail and antennae.

crawling casseroles from predators swimming above.

As Schwiebert had described years before, and as Edwards had recently reproduced so beautifully, the goldens have very distinctly banded abdomens. Finally, I observed how bulky the insect's legs are, and the dark, whip-like prominence of the tails and antennae.

Sitting down at the tying desk, my No. 1 priority was to recreate the wide, flattened silhouette of the golden stonefly nymph, and the graceful arc formed by this body as it drifts free in the current. With the latter in mind, I decided on the Tiemco 2302 for my hook. In addition to its subtle curvature, it also offers a wide gape and a suitably strong wire shank, two necessities when tying a large fly for use in heavy currents that have rocky bottoms.

Beadless version of the Salmonfly Biot Epoxy Stone Nymph pictured later, perfect for fishing shallow riffles.

The first time I saw one of Oliver Edwards's realistic golden stonefly nymphs, I just sat and stared, slack-jawed, a slight trickle of drool escaping my lips. *It looks better than the real thing.*

My first attempt to build a wide, flat underbody was with lead-free tying wire. I simply wrapped it around the hook as I would weight a standard nymph, then crushed it flat with a pair of non-serrated, flat-nosed pliers. Easy, right? Well, right…only problem was, the crushing part distorted the wire so that the "edges" of the wire abdomen were irregular and lumpy—thus any material wrapped over the top of it would be as well.

The second attempt, while slightly more involved, worked perfectly. I cut two lengths of the same non-toxic wire, each approximately twice the length of the hook shank, each with one end beveled at a gradual angle. I tied in the wires separately, one on each side of the shank, so that the beveled ends each terminated at a point just forward of the hook bend. Following this up with a bunch of thread wraps helped lock them into place; until they were totally lashed down, I found they could be manipulated into place with my fingers. I cut the excess wire off at about a mid-thorax position.

STEP 19

The finished fly.

In his book, *Flytyers Masterclass*, Oliver Edwards remarks that he doesn't particularly care for the wide goose biots used so prevalently on large stonefly nymphs. I couldn't agree more. While I do use biots, I prefer turkey to goose, and I'm careful to select the narrowest barbs on the spine—almost always located near the top end of the feather. These accurately imitate the actual insect's thin appendages, and are soft and supple when wet. I select a matched pair for the tail, tying one in on each side of the hook so the biots natural curvature flares outward. If the tails won't spread properly, I'll first dub a small ball where the non-toxic lead strips slope to meet the hook shank. When tied on in front of this ball, and wrapped back over until they push up against it, the tails are forced to flare.

Whereas I'd always thought of golden stone nymphs as being just smaller, lighter-colored versions of their aquatic roommate, the salmonfly, closer examination showed goldens possess a much flatter body profile.

Tied in jumbo sizes, the G. B. Biot Epoxy Golden Stone is a superb steelhead pattern, particularly when dead-drifted near the bottom, in fast, boulder-studded runs.

I've always loved these turkey biots. They're typically longer than their goose counterparts, allowing for additional revolutions while forming a body, which is convenient on larger flies. They're also ideal for tiny patterns. When wrapped, they create a glossy effect, as well as a naturally-ribbed segmentation. I use them for dries, nymphs, emergers—almost everything. So, I knew before I even started designing my golden stone what the abdomen would be tied with. On smaller versions, a single biot will suffice; on models larger than a size 12, you'll need to use two.

Begin by tying the biot in by the tip, right where the tapered non-toxic wire strips end. Coat the underbody with a thin layer of Flexament, and then wind the biot forward, overlapping slightly with each turn. The Flexament beneath the biots is a simple but critical step, and makes the difference between a one-fish pattern and a fly capable of lasting for dozens of trout. When you run out of feather, simply tie it off, attach another biot where the first one ended, and repeat the process. You'll probably want to lop off the tip of this second biot before tying it in, using only the remaining two-thirds of the feather; otherwise, the widths of the raised ribbed segments won't match up. Keep in mind that the abdomen should form

shorter), so they flare outwards, just as with the tail. Tie the thread off, and slide the bead forward over the thread wraps.

Reattach the thread where you left off, at the front of the abdomen. Tie in two identical slips of turkey tail, one directly on top of the other. I started using turkey tail for wing cases many years ago because of its dark, golden-brown color. I'll sometimes use a synthetic substitute, but rarely—few can capture an aquatic insect's natural dorsal mottling as well.

I've always loved these turkey biots. They're typically longer than their goose counterparts, allowing for additional revolutions while forming a body, which is convenient on larger flies. They're also ideal for tiny patterns.

about half the entire fly's length.

It's usually at this point that I like to tie in the antennae—any sooner and they get in my way constructing the rear half of the fly; any later and wraps of material can lock the metal bead in place against the hook eye, making them impossible to attach. Tie off the thread right here, in the middle of the fly, then reattach it immediately behind the hook eye. Slide the metal bead back as far as it will go, making room to tie in another matched pair of slim turkey biot tips (identical to the tail, but slightly

I chose to use dubbing for the thorax of this pattern for several reasons. First, it's easy to tie on a lot of the stuff, then simply sculpt it to the desired shape. Also, a bit picked out on the underside of the thorax does a credible job of imitating the actual golden's thoracic gill structures. Next, if the particular type of dubbing is chosen carefully, it will hold water very well, creating a fleshy, slightly translucent look.

Finally, I'm a huge believer in building my flies with many colors. When combined they create a dominant hue. Real insects, observed closely from a trout's-eye view, possess myriad colors; a golden stone looks brown and gold at a glance, but up close possesses many hue variations. Mixing my own dubbing blends enables me to more accurately duplicate this effect. Many wiser anglers believe that having several colors blended in body dubbing increases the odds of a fish seeing a shade they like. It's a theory I tend to adopt, though predicting the way a trout sees our offerings is an inexact science at best.

Finding the correct material for the fly's legs was a struggle for me. First I used round rubber. While still a good choice, it looked too artificial to me at the time.

Tied in a chocolate-brown color, the Biot Epoxy Nymph design becomes a deadly imitation of the nymphal salmonfly.

able and susceptible to fish. After allowing the glue to dry, I dubbed a narrow band to hide the wing-case tie-down, and also to take up the space between the thorax and metal bead.

For a final touch, I wanted to imitate the various mottling I saw on real goldens. Using a dark-brown waterproof marking pen, I splotched the back of the abdomen, dotted stripes on the tail and antennae, and completely covered the top 180 degrees of the dubbed head. *Voila!* Flattened profile, dark on top and golden beneath, distinctly banded abdomen, heavy legs, whip-like tails and antennae—sound familiar? Now for the trout's opinion.

The upper Sacramento below Dunsmuir ran high and clear, May runoff yielding grudgingly to June's perfection. I was logy from the 90° heat and the giant cheeseburger I'd sloppily engulfed on the drive up from Redding—it was tempting to just lie down under a towering pine next to the river and doze until evening, when the big stone dries would start flying. In fact that was exactly what I'd decided on, but when I took my mandatory walk down next to the water to take a look I changed my mind. Not only was the shoreline vegetation littered with the empty husks of hundreds of emerged stonefly nymphs, which I expected, but there were actu-

I'm a huge believer in building my flies with many colors. When combined they create a dominant hue. Real insects, observed closely from a trout's-eye view, possess myriad colors; a golden stone looks brown and gold at a glance, but up close possesses many hue variations.

Next I tried knotted biots, but gave up on that as simply too time consuming; they were also a bit stiff in the water, though they looked fantastic in the vise.

Finally, I hit upon laying a mottled hen hackle on top of the thorax. This way, when the wing cases were pulled over the top, the soft, undulating, speckled "legs" extended out to the sides. For those crazies like me who like to build in all the bells and whistles, a neat little trick is to carefully groom small segments out of each side of the hen feather before covering it with the turkey. This creates the illusion of individual legs. While perhaps more impressive in shadowboxes than on tippets, it is undeniably cool.

After pulling the wing cases forward and tying them down in front of the thorax, I coated the turkey with epoxy. This suggested the ready-to-pop look of an emerger heading for the bank to undergo metamorphosis, the point at which stonefly nymphs tend to be the most avail-

ally legions of the live critters creeping clumsily through the streamside grasses, as well. Holy cow! I'd never actually seen anything like this before, and I realized that if there were hundreds of bugs crawling on land, there must be thousands doing the same thing under the water.

Golden stonefly nymphs, I knew, often emerge en masse; trout commonly capitalize on this phenomenon by taking up residence within a few feet of shore, plucking them off the streambed rocks like ripe cherries. Bankside willows and undergrowth made fishing from the shore impossible, so, cinching up my wading belt, I cautiously shuffled my way to midstream. Hanging one of my new golden stone nymphs a yard beneath a large yarn indicator, I began plying the pockets and slots near the bank. Almost immediately I got a vicious take, plunging my indicator from view. An equally violent response on my part launched a 10-inch missile on a deadly path toward my cranium; fortunately, the undersized rainbow missed by an eyelash, came unattached in mid-flight, and re-entered its own atmosphere unscathed.

I can only imagine what must have gone through his little mind—I'm guessing he's getting by on mayflies and caddisflies these days.

An equally violent response on my part launched a 10-inch missile on a deadly path toward my cranium; fortunately, the undersized rainbow missed by an eyelash, came unattached in mid-flight, and re-entered its own atmosphere unscathed.

Reduce abdomen width, substitute pheasant-tail fiber antennae, and tie in a dark-brown hue for a superb little dark stone pattern. I like to drop it behind a large golden.

The next pull-down was much more subtle, but when I came tight, whatever it was snapped my tippet on the first headshake. *All-righty, then!* With shaking fingers I drew the 2X from my pack, knotted a length to the indicator, and tied on my last new nymph.

Probably the fish would have hammered any old golden stonefly pattern that day, but they definitely had eyes for mine. By the time the adults started fluttering from the trees that evening, I could not have cared less—I fished the nymph until I couldn't see the bank, much less my indicator, finally stopping only because the nighttime wading started getting a little hairy. Driving home that night, my mind was filled with memories from the afternoon. As I relived each riffle, plunging indicator, and catapulting trout, I became more excited about trying my fly in other waters. For me, a new "confidence" fly had been born.

CHAPTER 9

SAC FRY

11:59 p.m. NEW YEAR'S EVE: *On the television, Dick Clark narrates the sinking ball, celebratory shots can be heard popping outside, confetti is strewn about the living-room floor, and I . . . well, I am at my tying desk trying to put the finishing touches on a brand-new pattern I'd thought up just hours before. Man, I think I'm taking this hobby a little too seriously.*

3:20 p.m. (earlier that afternoon): I couldn't help myself, though. That morning I'd been given a pickled, progressive display showing each life-stage of the king salmon, from newly-laid egg to the several-inches-long smolt prepared to migrate downstream to the ocean. The varying egg metamorphoses were garnering most of my attention; studying them made me realize just how little thought I'd given to their various stages of maturation.

SAC FRY

RECIPE

HOOK: TMC 2457, size 12

THREAD: 3/0 white Monocord or equivalent

BODY TUBING:
Tan Ultra Lace Tubing

BODY INSERT AND TAIL:
Pearl Angel Hair

EGG SAC: Glo Bug Yarn or equivalent, your choice of color

EYES: Silver prismatic 3-D stick-on eyes

EPOXY: Devcon 5 Minute Epoxy or equivalent

DANVILLE'S
3/0
100 YDS.

WAXED
MONOCORD

Cut a short (approximately 3/4 of an inch) length of tan tubing. Push a wire bobbin threader through it, so that the end sticks well out one end. Insert a sparse clump of pearl Angel Hair into the end of the threader.

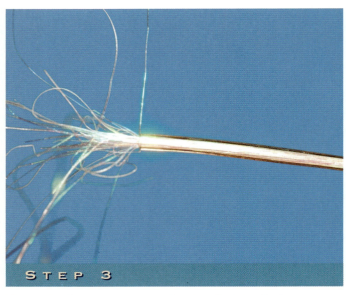

Once the threader has completely exited the tubing a short distance, trim the Angel Hair between the tip of the threader and the tubing—this abbreviated clump will form the "tail" at the end of the Sac Fry's body. Trim the Angel Hair at the other end flush with the tubing.

Pull the threader back into the tubing, drawing the Angel Hair with it.

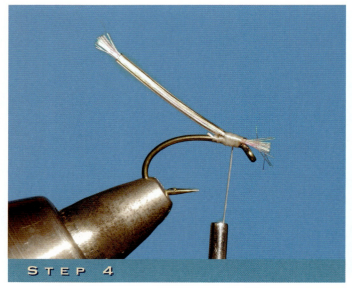

Form a thread base just behind the eye of the hook—remember, most of the hook shank will not be utilized with this pattern. Tie in the preformed body just behind the hook eye. You'll notice the tubing usually has a natural curvature to it—tie the body in so that it curves upward between the hook shank and the tail.

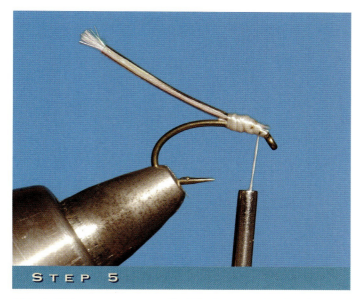

Use thread wraps to cover all of the loose ends of tubing and Angel Hair right behind the hook eye. Unlike most trout flies you'll ever tie, go ahead and strive for a bulky build-up of thread here—it forms a larger, more desirable base to attach your stick-on eyes to.

Take a short length of egg yarn and fold it over, creating a "solid loop"—a teardrop-shaped loop with no open space in the middle. Tie this loop in beneath the hook shank so that the folded end faces rearward. The yarn loop should be long and bulky enough so that, if pushed upward against the hook shank, it covers virtually the entire remaining bare hook. Again, thread build-up while tying this yarn in is a good thing! Whip-finish and clip your thread.

Like most anglers, I'd always been content to use simple pink or orange egg imitations—I now realized the trout were seeing a lot more involved variations on those themes. As I perused the other stages, my eye was drawn repeatedly to the sac fry. I wasn't sure why, but I found something about it intriguing. Then it dawned on me: While I'd tied dozens of variations of eggs, and more than a few smolt patterns, I'd never considered the sac-fry stage. In fact, I'd never even seen a fly designed specifically for it.

The more I thought about this, the more excited I became. Here was a prominent food source present wherever trout and spawning salmon coexist, yet few if any fly-fishers were taking advantage of it. Moreover, if the old adage, "50 days at 50 degrees" (the average time in optimum conditions between the eggs being laid and the sac fry's emergence from the gravel) was correct, then the fat rainbows in the lower Sacramento River behind my house should be gorging on them at that very moment. If my conclusion was accurate, this could be like discovering a new major insect hatch on a familiar stream—in other words, nearly unthinkable. I'd already planned a drift on the river the next day, figuring most people would be sleeping late and nursing hangovers—now I had a chance to turn it into a truly exciting experiment. But first, I'd need a fly.

> **Then it dawned on me: While I'd tied dozens of variations of eggs, and more than a few smolt patterns, I'd never considered the sac-fry stage.**

5:45 p.m: As I studied my preserved sample, one feature became immediately obvious—freshly-emerged salmon are more sac than fry. What's more, the disproportionately large protein masses are not round, like an egg, but rather oblong, extending along the fry's belly. I decided this pattern would have to be more like an egg with a little streamer attached, rather than vice versa; therefore, the most appropriate hook choice would be one suitable for an egg fly. I settled on the TMC 2457 with its short shank, wide gape, and wickedly sharp point.

6:10 p.m: My choice of materials to emulate the egg sac would be crucial, as this was probably the single most important trigger on the fly. I was sure I had the perfect answer, though, in using an orange-colored, translucent plastic bead. A trip to the local craft store supplied the ideal color. As I sat back down at my desk I had already devised two possible methods of attaching it.

The first, stringing it onto a piece of monofilament then tying the two ends of the line down, didn't work out quite as planned, as the bead took up nearly the entire hooking gape. Idea No. 2, melting the bead to the underside

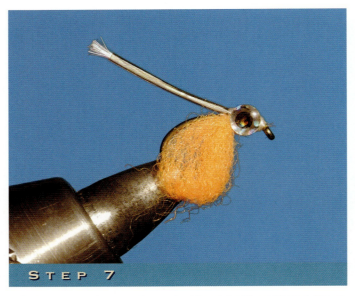

STEP 7

STEP 9

Attach one stick-on eye to each side of the thread head. There should be just a slight bit of the thread-covered shank showing between the hook eye and the forward edge of the eyes. I find putting a drop of epoxy or super glue onto the backs of the eyes before sticking them in place helpful—otherwise, they tend to move around during the next step, when you cover the head with epoxy.

The finished Sac Fry.

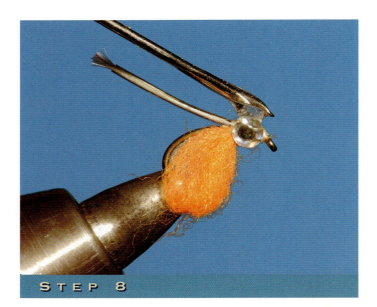

STEP 8

Use a fine-tipped bodkin or needle to apply 5 Minute Epoxy to the head of the fly. I generally coat the entire head, essentially forming a round "bubble" of epoxy encompassing the head and eyes. If you prefer not to coat the face of the stick-on eyes with epoxy, you can choose to simply fill in the gaps on the top and bottom of the head, between the thread base and the inner, flat surfaces of the eyes. This is a bit more tedious, but some may prefer the finished look.

of the hook, took up less gape, but when I had it in place, I realized the bead was round and in no way resembled the oval shape of an actual sac. Back to the drawing board.

Finally, after ruling out hot glue as being too hard in texture, the obvious came to me. What did I use to tie my egg flies? Egg yarn, of course. So, after finding the correct color to match my sample, I took a length of the yarn (only a small percentage of a single strand actually, to avoid excess bulk), folded it over on itself into a

tied on they were wonderful, translucent without bulk. Unfortunately, with any handling they quickly became mangled and decidedly unrealistic. Marabou was my next choice, but it "blossomed" when dead-drifted in water, not even vaguely resembling the actual fry's profile.

Finally, I got it. A short piece of clear, hollow plastic tubing gave me a remarkably accurate body silhouette, albeit a bit of a lifeless one. I remedied this last issue by using a wire bobbin threader to pull a hank of pearl Angel

Finally, I got it. A short piece of clear, hollow plastic tubing gave me a remarkably accurate body silhouette, albeit a bit of a lifeless one. I remedied this last issue by using a wire bobbin threader to pull a hank of pearl Angel Hair through the tubing.

stretched-out, oblong loop, then tied it on just behind and underneath the hook eye. When immersed in the water, this yarn becomes a virtual egg sac, both visually and to the touch. Simple, and perfect.

9:45 p.m: The TV is on, and as I tie I'm forced to rehash all of the day's college games, which I would rather have just watched—when does the real New Year's show start?

You almost have to look twice to see the bodies on these little fish—they are incredibly slim and largely transparent. I originally tried imitating this with several strands of flash laid over the top of the hook. When first

Hair through the tubing. Not only did this lend the body a superb realism, but when I accidentally allowed a short clump to extend out the rear, it flared slightly, creating an extraordinary facsimile of a newborn salmon's tail.

A note on this body: My suggestion to you is to leave it alone, as is. If, however, you're a compulsive tinkerer like me, you can add a few more details with waterproof marking pens: tan on the top portion of the fly, tiny olive spots along the flanks. You might even thread a single strand of orange Krystal Flash through the tubing, with the Angel Hair (check out an actual sac fry—they have a threadlike bloodstripe running most the length of their bodies).

Do these additions make the fly look unbelievably cool? Like you can't imagine. Will they catch you even one more fish? Get serious—even I know better than that. I just can't help myself.

11:05 p.m: O-Town *is harmonizing their latest smash hit on the small screen (did I mention this was a few years ago?), and I'm starting to get a little rummy, but I'm on the home stretch now.*

The way I figure it, there's only one more triggering feature of consequence that needs to be added: the prominent, unwaveringly panic-stricken eyes bugging out of these little guys' heads. I started by pasting on plain black-and-white stick-on eyes, and they looked—well,

he didn't immediately tie one on as we waded into our positions. *Just wait,* I thought.

As it turns out, waiting is exactly what I did. Despite having subtly managed to procure the best water for myself (Jim has on occasion rather ungenerously pointed out this supposed character flaw to me), my hookup total after 20 minutes was hovering somewhere between zero and zip.

Jim, on the other hand, was landing fish on his clearly inferior egg pattern with annoying regularity. *What am I missing?* I asked myself. The heavy, riffled chute I was stationed on was perfect. Not actually a spawning area, it was a spot where loose eggs from upstream spawners were constantly funneled—I knew trout held there. Doubts

A note on this body: My suggestion to you is to leave it alone, as is. If, however, you're a compulsive tinkerer like me, you can add a few more details with waterproof marking pens.

plain. Closer examination of the naturals revealed distinctly silver outer eyes with black pupils, so I dug around and found some silver holographic models. As I turned this new version around in my vise, I felt a thrill of anticipation: It looked real! Finally, to lock the eyes in place, and to simulate the fry's slightly enlarged head, I covered everything between the hook eye and the yolk sac with 5 Minute Epoxy.

12:40 a.m: The ball has fallen, and I'm shot.

Fortunately, this new pattern was one of my simpler ones, and I'd cranked out half a dozen in short order once I'd arrived at my final design. I fell asleep satisfied, with visions of heavy-shouldered rainbows dancing in my head.

We launched the drift boat into a cold winter fog, quickly oaring downstream to a known salmon-spawning riffle. High-stepping out over the gunwales, we grabbed our rods as the muffled sounds of active salmon on their redds drifted through the mist. Experience taught us two important lessons: First and most important, do not wade out into the salmon. Doing so would mean walking right on top of their nests, where each step would prove catastrophic, crushing first dozens, then hundreds and even thousands of the eggs and immature salmon buried or seeking refuge in the gravelly streambed. Even a small handful of thoughtless anglers can seriously impact a river's many future salmon generations. Besides, the jockeying, rooster-tailing giants were right in front of us.

The second lesson we'd learned was that trout often throw caution to the wind when it comes to egg-laying salmon, moving into ridiculously shallow water to take advantage of the drifting orange morsels.

I'd already shown Jim my newest creation. He'd nodded along as I enthusiastically explained my theory about this unbelievably overlooked food source, but I noticed

Look like a cartoon character? Guess what? So does the real thing! Wraith-like body, outsized neon egg sac and bulging holographic eyes accurately describe either the natural or its emulator. You can bet the fish aren't laughing.

started to creep into my mind. Maybe I had it all wrong. Maybe the trout liked eggs so much they just ignored the little salmonids. Maybe...and then it happened. I'd shuffled my way downstream a bit, so my casts were now fanning out over actual mogulled redds, when suddenly my indicator went down with cartoon-like force, actually making a soft "popping" sound as it was yanked savagely under and upstream.

I almost giggled, it was so outrageously violent—I'd never seen a take like it. My astonishment turned quickly to concern, however, when the unseen predator robbed me of even the chance to set the hook, instead slamming

I was still totally out of control when the fish swapped ends, not just running but leaping straight back at me, each panicked breach bringing it closer and closer, and introducing more and more slack into my line.

my rod tip to the water and gaining downstream momentum at an alarming rate of speed. I was still totally out of control when the fish swapped ends, not just running but leaping straight back at me, each panicked breach bringing it closer and closer, and introducing more and more slack into my line.

I gave up. The fish was still on, but it had so badly humiliated me that I just dropped my rod and began laughing out loud. Jim, too, it seemed, was enjoying my brutal drubbing—as I looked downstream, he was doubled over, tears streaming down his face, pointing derisively at the trout which, though now unhooked, had continued its frantic leaps unabated.

"Nice job!" he managed to wheeze through racking shudders. "What'd he take?"

Only then did I remember just exactly what it *had* eaten: my sac fry! I still count the rest of that day as one of my more memorable spent on the water, simply for the sheer excitement and satisfaction of having an idea come wonderfully to fruition. Did I catch more than Jim, who continued using eggs and nymphs? No, but I held my own. And that, along with a continued string of absolutely vicious strikes, remains permanently etched in my memory.

I've enjoyed many successful outings with this little fish pattern since that first adventure. While I remain somewhat mystified over the disproportionately aggressive takes it seems to provoke, I have made several useful observations.

First, trout seem to prefer this fly when presented in and around spawning redds, or in the deeper runs immediately below. This makes sense, when you realize sac fry actually spend most of their early days buried in, or swimming immediately above, these cobbled nests.

Second, remember that, being encumbered with such outsized egg sacs, salmon fry aren't particularly agile swimmers. Consequently, unlike many baitfish techniques, a dead-drift nymphing presentation is often the most effective. I prefer to fish the sac fry beneath an indicator, allowing long, uninterrupted presentations, though tight-line swinging one through a run can produce some unforgettable grabs.

Finally, in most rivers, fish seem to key into this "hatch" for specific windows of time, then largely ignore them for other, more plentiful, food sources.

My friend Cory Williams keyed me into a neat little secret about knowing when the time was right—he discovered that trout aren't the only ones eating this life stage. Several different species of diving ducks also forage on them, sometimes seemingly specifically. Using Cory's advice, I found these ducks to be unerring indicators of the presence of sac fry, often observing them surfacing with silvery mouthfuls of the diminutive fish. When the fry matured, became more difficult to catch and moved on, so did the ducks. Perhaps the most accurate predictor of their residency, however, is to research a river's spawning cycles. When salmon are paired up and begin to actually lay and fertilize their eggs (not to be confused with the process of nest building, which precedes the fertilized egg process), mark the date on your calendar. In approximately two months there *will* be sac fry in the water, though in my experience fish will start reacting to them soon after spawning begins.

Are fish simply mistaking this pattern for a drifting egg, as some have suggested? I doubt it. I've seen far too many occasions where trout would eat this fly aggressively while spurning egg patterns, and the opposite as well. And fished side by side, the egg is normally mouthed softly, while sac fry induce furious inhalations. No, this is a tangible event. If you live near a river where trout and spawning salmon live together, you owe it to yourself to take advantage.

RAG HEX NYMPH

MENTION *HEXAGENIA* TO A FLY FISHER IN CALIFORNIA and he's likely to nod vaguely, perhaps remembering something about "Michigan Caddis," those giant bugs that hatch so profusely from the Great Lakes that automobiles skid uncontrollably on roads slicked with their carcasses. Rarely have I encountered an angler who realizes these magnum mayflies are also scattered throughout the West, with numerous lakes and spring creeks hosting reliable nocturnal emergences each summer. For those anglers who are onto the Hex, they represent an incredible opportunity to fish huge nymphs and dry flies for what are invariably the largest fish in any given body of water. Since here on the West Coast these "Hex hotels" are spread a little thin, hitting one at its prime usually involves some traveling.

RAG HEX NYMPH

RECIPE

HOOK: TMC 2457, size 6-10

THREAD: Tan UNI 8/0

TAIL: Natural gray ostrich-herl tips

ABDOMEN: Gold EZE Bug Yarn

GILLS: Natural gray marabou

THORAX: Ginger Buggy Nymph dubbing or equivalent

LEGS: Pumpkin barred Nymph Sili-Legs

WING CASE: Mottled dark golden-brown turkey tail

WING CASE GLOSS: Devcon 5 Minute Epoxy

EYES: Black bead chain

MARKING PEN: Waterproof ink, light tan or gold

STEP 1

Cut a piece of EZE Bug yarn two to two and a half inches in length (about twice the actual length of the finished abdomen). About half an inch from one end of the yarn, peel the fibers apart to expose the braided cores; with each end of the yarn held between separate fingers on either hand, use your bobbin to make six to 10 wraps of thread in this small area. It takes a little practice—once you get a couple of wraps in place you can release the bobbin and just twirl the remaining wraps using centrifugal force

STEP 3

Trim the longer fibers of the abdomen short, so that only a shaved core remains.

STEP 2

Release the longer end of the yarn. Pick up three evenly matched ostrich-herl tips between your thumb and forefinger. Grasping the longer yarn end between your middle finger and palm (or however is most comfortable to you), use your thumb and forefinger to lay the tips on top of the yarn, so that the tips extending over the tie-down area are the length you desire for the finished tail. As a general rule, the ostrich tails will be approximately the same length as the fly's abdomen. Using the "twirling bobbin" method described above, secure the tails to the yarn with another four to six wraps of thread, and then use a hand whip finish to tie off. Clip off the butt ends of the ostrich, and all of the yarn behind the thread tie-down. A drop of Flexament on the thread wraps will lock the tails into place.

STEP 4

Attach your abdomen/tail assembly (preferably so the tails have an upward cant) to the hook shank at a point just forward of the hook bend, wrapping forward over the yarn until about three-quarters of the hook shank has been covered. Trim the excess.

STEP 5

Tie in the black bead chain just forward of where the yarn tie-down ends, using a figure-eight wrap.

Though normally I prefer to fish with a friend, there is a certain, free-spirited exhilaration associated with a trout-fishing road trip alone. The anticipation of moving at one's own pace; the freedom to eat dinner (and breakfast) at the gas station mini-mart; the sovereignty to stay up late at the crummy little motel watching wonderfully awful science fiction movies starring wildy screaming women and rubber-suited monsters; and sleeping in as late as you darn well please. Perhaps best of all, on the drive there, you can listen to whatever music you desire, even some of that crazy weird stuff you really don't want anyone knowing you like. So it was that I found myself

Trout's-eye view of this monster mayfly nymph. Now imagine it jigging, breathing and undulating through the water!

There is a certain, free-spirited exhilaration associated with a trout-fishing road trip alone. The sovereignty to stay up late at the crummy little motel watching wonderfully awful science fiction movies starring wildy screaming women and rubber-suited monsters.

recently, companionless, on a six-hour drive to a little spring creek reputed to have this most elusive of hatches. With a CD player blaring and all my windows wide open, I shamelessly indulged a preference for harmonics that "eclectic" probably doesn't quite cover, at a decibel level perhaps best suited to a junior high school pep rally. I crooned with the dulcet, velvet-throated Nat King Cole; felt gooseflesh as Elvis commanded his American Trilogy; commiserated with Waylon and Willie about moving back to Luckenbach, Texas; and felt hot tears of emotion listening to Whitney Houston belt out the Star Spangled Banner, at octaves few other humans can achieve.

Honest to God, I gotta get out more.

I felt that old, delicious nervousness in my stomach as I pulled off the main highway onto an unfamiliar dirt road, eager to catch my first glimpse of a stream I'd only heard about. The butterflies turned to outright apprehension,

STEP 6

Peel a sparse clump of marabou fibers from the stem of a blood feather, then use a "pinch-and-tear" method to even the tips. Secure the fibers on the far side of the hook, wrapping over the material so that it butts up against the EZE Bug—these gills should be approximately one-half the length of the abdomen. Repeat the process on the near side of the hook.

STEP 7

Tie in a slip of turkey tail so that it extends back over the abdomen.

STEP 9

Form a dubbing loop, with a dubbing twister inserted into the bottom of the loop. Insert clumps of dubbing down the length of the loop.

STEP 8

Repeat the process, so that the second slip lies over the top of the first.

STEP 10

Use the twister to spin the loop into a dubbing "brush." Be careful when twirling the dubbing twister, as the gills have a tendency to get sucked into the process—moistening them slightly and stroking them back against the abdomen will help keep them out of the way.

STEP 11

When the dubbing brush is finished, wrap it forward to form the thorax. Coax the dubbed fibers rearward with thumb and fingers after each revolution, to ensure you don't continually wrap over the top of a lot of bulk. When you reach a spot just behind the bead-chain eyes, tie the loop off and trim the excess.

STEP 12

Use a dubbing teaser to pick fibers out to the sides, on both the top and bottom of the thorax. You want a thorax profile that is just slightly wider than the abdomen. Trim the top of the thorax fairly short and the bottom only slightly—there should be more dubbing bulk on the bottom. Trim the sides of the thorax as necessary, both to eliminate any long, straggly hairs, and to make sure an even amount will protrude out either side of the wing case.

however, as the trail quickly deteriorated in the approaching twilight. Suddenly, I found myself in that uncomfortable place between needing to put 'er into four-wheel drive, and not being exactly sure that will even be enough. Just as I began to panic (my brain blending *Deliverance, Texas Chain Saw Massacre,* and *The Hills Have Eyes*), the forest opened before me: There it was. It wasn't quite dusk, so I could still make out the flat-watered creek wending its serpentine route through a grassy valley. It looked so small—*could I have come to the wrong stream?* Parking at the meadow's edge, I picked my way cautiously to the water, using the truck's headlights to avoid marshy spots that would soak my only pair of shoes.

The extended EZE Bug abdomen idea can be used as a template for many other patterns, such as this Rag Golden Stone Nymph.

> **Standing at the stream's threshold, I quickly concluded I was right where I belonged, listening with sublime joy to the soul-stirring rhythm of finned predators exploding on haplessly drifting prey.**

Standing at the stream's threshold, I quickly concluded I was right where I belonged, listening with sublime joy to the soul-stirring rhythm of finned predators exploding on haplessly drifting prey. The insects had to be *Hexagenias*. Knowing I'd never get my gear rigged in the failing light, and that I still needed to set up camp, I reluctantly made my way back to the truck.

The next morning was glorious: sunlit and warm without another camper, or angler, in sight. After a filling breakfast of cold Pop-Tarts and Gatorade, I grabbed my rod, shouldered my vest, and wandered down to where the two-mile-long pasture emerged from the trees. The creek was mud and gravel, with alluring undercut banks and deep, mysterious pools. I knew there'd be no Hexes until after sundown but, as is often the case with new water, my fingers were trembling with expectation as I knotted on a small parachute and drifted it down a perfect current seam. The quiet, confident slurp still caught

STEP 13

Pull each of the turkey-tail wing cases forward over the thorax, tying them down individually, one directly on top of the other.

STEP 15

Tie in a length of Sili Legs, wrapping back over it until it is snugged up against the turkey wing cases.

STEP 14

After both have been secured in front of the thorax, pull them both back over the thorax at the same time. Wrap back over them, to lock them into a rearward facing position.

STEP 16

Dub a head, using either a dubbing loop or standard twist-on technique. I find the loop style to be unnecessary here, and more time consuming than it's worth. This "head" section should be narrower than the thorax, although I like to figure-eight around the bead chain eyes several times to build some bulk.

STEP 17

Pull both wing cases forward individually again, securing them in front of the bead-chain eyes and just behind the eye of the hook. Trim the excess. Trim the legs so that if pressed against the body, they reach to about the ends of the gill fibers. Tie the fly off.

STEP 18

Using a tan waterproof marking pen, color the entire dorsal surface of the abdomen, so that it is a markedly darker hue than the belly. Do the same for the dubbed thorax that protrudes out each side of the wing case, taking care to mark only the top fibers.

me by surprise, and I nearly decapitated the poor little dinker with my overzealous strike.

Oh-oh, I remember thinking—the infamous fish-on-the-first-cast jinx!

I needn't have worried. Each inviting pocket produced another undersized rainbow or brown. I wasn't complaining; the fish were jewel-like in appearance and aggressive to a fault. Still, I couldn't help wondering what had happened to the larger fish I had heard rising the night before. But as I am easy to please and was mostly looking ahead to the evening's emergence, it took me until later that afternoon to figure things out: The larger fish had to be glutting on the nighttime *Hexagenias*. They were hiding out during the midday hours! This revelation was only briefly encouraging, however, as I realized this would leave me with three more 12-hour days of eight-inch trout, each session capped by an all-too-rushed 30-minute glimpse of the fishing I'd actually come for.

The writer described the outlandish densities of burrowing Hex nymphs found in areas where nocturnal hatches were observed. If these nymphs were so plentiful, wouldn't it make sense that trout would be on the lookout for them constantly during the few short weeks of the insects' annual emergence?

Something occurred to me then, a fact I'd read years earlier in a fishing-oriented entomology book. The writer described the outlandish densities of burrowing Hex nymphs found in areas where nocturnal hatches were observed, sometimes as many as 500 specimens per square foot of stream bottom! The book went on to depict *en masse* emergences in late afternoons that incited wild nymph feeding orgies. Often, it stated, trout would become so gorged on these wriggling hordes, they'd ignore the subsequent floating duns altogether. *Hmmm.* If these nymphs were so plentiful, wouldn't it make sense that trout would be on the lookout for them constantly during the few short weeks of the insects' annual emergence, even eager to pick off stragglers any time during the day?

Though loaded with truckloads of floating imitations, I didn't own a single nymph even vaguely resembling that of the subsurface Hex. Pawing through my boxes, I discovered several marabou leeches that were the right size, though, and were a natural gray color that seemed like it might just be close enough. I switched to a sinking line, determined to dredge the flies along the bottom of every fishy-looking run in the creek; I knew the nymphs were burrowers, so this seemed to make the most sense. With

Before applying the epoxy coating to the wing case, look closely to make sure no loose hairs will be covered—it's not a big deal, but a stray filament will mar the finished, high-gloss effect. After mixing the epoxy, use a dubbing needle to plop a big drop of it right in the middle of the wing case. Use the tip of the needle to distribute epoxy to every bit of the turkey, right out to the edges. Don't worry here if the epoxy is a little thin, or isn't perfectly glossy. Apply another large drop, again right in the middle, but this time do not touch it with the needle; as you watch, it will self-level, giving your wing case a realistic, shiny look.

Finished Rag Hex Nymph.

renewed enthusiasm, I marched down the stream, casting across and down, letting the line sweep the "nymph" through one deep run after another. After another. After another.

My big revelation obviously wasn't working. As my confidence deflated like a month-old helium balloon forgotten behind the couch, I struggled for an answer. Nothing was coming to me, so I finally decided the sinking line swinging through the holes must be spooking the fish (lame, I know, but desperation routinely clouds my already questionable judgment). I switched back to a floating line and added split shot to get the fly down. The creek's currents weren't fast enough to accommodate a traditional up-and-across, dead-drift presentation, so I cast across, waited until I felt a bottom bump, then started a moderately fast, short-strip retrieve.

> **My big revelation obviously wasn't working. As my confidence deflated like a month-old helium balloon forgotten behind the couch, I struggled for an answer. Nothing was coming to me, so I finally decided the sinking line swinging through the holes must be spooking the fish**

Within an hour I'd had half a dozen grabs. I had hooked and landed half of those, including my first two big trout. I was onto something—but hadn't a clue what.

Same fly, same water, both techniques presenting the fly near the bottom. I considered that maybe my first theory *had* been correct, but by now even I was dubious of that bit of insight, as I'd personally caught thousands of supposedly sophisticated spring-creek trout on sinking lines over the years. So what could it be? Finally, I considered what the fly must have looked like to the fish, first while being swung slowly and smoothly through their living rooms on the sinking line, then hopped along the bottom like a jig.

Like a jig…that was it!

I also remembered reading a description of the motion of the emerging Hex nymph, describing a dramatic up-and-down undulation: very unlike the sinking line swing, but very much like the "hopping" induced by the split shot on my leader, being pulled upward by the floating line.

I didn't touch a dry fly for the next three days, save for the frantic evening frenzies brought on by the "twilight bombers," as I came to think of them. These nights were certainly the highlight of the trip, but no more satisfying than the consistent action I enjoyed with the nymphed leeches during the days. And I couldn't wait to get home and come up with a better pattern.

First things first: which hook? I had always loved the

concept of jointed "wiggle flies" for large nymphs, and knew this was the direction I would pursue. I needed a short-shank hook that would function as the forward half of the fly. I recognized that many trout caught on a Hex nymph would be sizable, and that many fly fishers in the Great Lakes region routinely use these nymphs for steelhead and even king salmon. The TMC 2457 became my hook of choice, as it is needle-sharp, can handle large fish on heavy tippets, and comes in appropriately large sizes. I

materials guru Hugh Beglin, the guy who brought us Estaz, among other notable staples for the contemporary fly tier. Hugh was very animated in his excitement over a new material he had discovered—would I mind giving it a try? This was kind of like asking a lion if he'd mind sharing his space with a gazelle. Forty-eight hours later I was tearing open his expressed package.

To be fair, my initial reaction was short of enthusiastic. In fact, I took another look, to make sure I'd gotten the

Hugh was very animated in his excitement over a new material he had discovered—would I mind giving it a try? This was kind of like asking a lion if he'd mind sharing his space with a gazelle.

find a No. 8 to be the perfect average dimension, but Nos. 6 and 10 can also be useful from one fishery to another.

Now the hard part: How to construct the extended body? Other tiers had fashioned effective versions utilizing abdomens tied on wire or hook-shank undercarriages, but I always felt they were a little stiff and prone to fouling on the hook. Also, they invariably had a gap between the thorax and abdomen, which while apparently not bothering trout much, looked intuitively wrong to my eye.

Then serendipity stepped in. I was contacted by

right box. Inside were several small Ziploc bags, each filled with lengths of a fuzzy yarn strikingly similar to what I'd recently observed in the local craft store's bargain baskets. Absolutely nothing remarkable-looking about it at all. But I have a hard and fast rule that the true measure of a fly—or tying material—is what it looks like wet. I always remind myself of this truism when I come up with a fly that looks terrific in the vise but has never seen water. In this case, given Hugh's track record, I decided I couldn't write off his discovery without first seeing what it looked like from a fish's perspective.

Boy, was that the right decision! My first experiments working with the material (Hugh named it EZE Bug) were a little rough but, from the moment I dunked my first prototype under the kitchen faucet to saturate it, I was mesmerized. When allowed to soak up water, a simple two-inch segment of this stuff looks alive, as if it might sprout legs and creep away. What had looked totally unimpressive dry, metamorphosed magically into a mottled, fleshy, 3-D "creature" when wet. I madly began devising ways to utilize this remarkable new stuff.

So it was a few short weeks later that I sat down to my vise, certain I had the perfect answer to my Hex-abdomen puzzle. My first model simply had a length of the yarn lashed to the hook. I knew it was too fat to accurately imitate a Hex nymph, but it looked so cool in the water. Fortunately, I figured out that the core of the material was three tightly twisted strands of string, each with its own protruding fluff—this meant that I could simply trim the fluff down close to the core, creating whatever taper

call: natural gray marabou, tied in at each side of, and pinched to a length just less than, the EZE Bug abdomen. When the fly is retrieved in an up-and-down motion, the marabou breathes enticingly. It drives fish nuts.

Like other mayflies, when Hex nymphs prepare to emerge, their wing cases darken and swell as a prelude to the wings bursting out (and burst is the operative word: on quiet nights the moment of transformation can sometimes actually be heard as a faint "pop," due to the size of the insect and the relative violence of the event). To emulate this, I chose to use a darkly mottled turkey tail slip, coated with a veneer of 5 Minute Epoxy. Actually, I recommend using two identical slips, one laid right on top of the other. This way, if the first feather splits, showing the dubbed thorax beneath, the second will give a solid foundation to spread the epoxy on; otherwise, the glue can soak into the thorax, ruining the fly.

As for the thorax itself, I decided to use a loop-dubbed technique. The Hex is a big bug. This method

> **What had looked totally unimpressive dry, metamorphosed magically into a mottled, fleshy, 3-D "creature" when wet. I madly began devising ways to utilize this remarkable new stuff.**

I desired. My pattern now looked good in the water and was anatomically correct. Success.

Not so fast. Unfortunately, within a dozen casts I watched that perfect taper disintegrate into something resembling Elmer Fudd's exploding shotgun. Turns out the triple-twisted strands aren't so tight once they get wet. My original solution was a drop of super glue at the tip of the body. This worked but looked a little messy. And sometimes the strands loosened up a bit behind the glue. I found that by simply wrapping several winds of thread around a given spot on the yarn's core, then hand whip-finishing at the same spot, the EZE Bug "abdomens" would never unravel.

Still, when tied to the hook, the body seemed to be missing something. Tails! Real Hex nymphs have very pronounced, hair-fringed tails, appendages that wave seductively as the insects migrate to the surface. So I simply laid in three evenly matched, natural-gray ostrich-herl tips as I did my core tie-down. After the whip finish, I trimmed away all of the EZE Bug left behind the tails, as well as the butt ends of the herls. *Now* I had the perfect extended Hex body: one that swam in an undulating manner in the water, rarely fouled on the hook, and showed no gap between the thorax and abdomen.

Hex nymph gills, befitting the outsized nature of the insect, are almost abnormally prominent. They're important to the Hex nymphs because they circulate air through the tight mud burrows the bugs live in. They're important to the fish because they provide yet another undulating trigger for them to key on. This wasn't a tough

allows the simple construction of a bulky, sculpting-friendly forward body. Because *Hexagenias* are so long and jointed, I also made the thorax a two-part affair: tie in the wing cases, form the dubbing loop, and wrap it forward about halfway to the eye of the hook. Next, bring the turkey forward and tie it down in front of the thorax, then pull the slips back over the wing case with your fingers. Tie the thread back over the feathers slightly. I can't emphasize too strongly how animated Hex nymphs are in the water. For this reason, I chose to tie in a single set of legs at this point. Because almost nothing in nature is monotonous in color, I chose to use barred Sili-Legs. They display the mottled camouflage that helps keep many actual critters alive, and they add wonderful motion.

I don't particularly enjoy using split-shot in a moderately paced chalk stream, so I knew that one feature of my new pattern was going to be weighted eyes. I had tied a few Hex nymphs in the past, mostly just for show, and had always liked the way burnt monofilament eyes had looked—just like the pictures of the actual nymphs in the book. Tim Fox, my friend and fellow fly innovator, had been telling me for ages that I needed to substitute black bead chain on them, that they were perfect for the fly and made the patterns fish better. Did I listen? Here again I was reminded why I need to pay more attention to Tim. Finally heeding his advice, I added the painted metal eyes. They're heavy enough to give the nymph a subtle yet distinct jigging motion, but aren't so ponderous as to dredge the bottom constantly. This is important. In my experience, trout tend to key in on this insect in the middle depths more than in the streambed.

Finish wrapping the rest of the dubbed thorax forward, figure-eight around the bead chain, then pull the wing cases over the top and secure them just behind the hook eye. Coat wing cases with epoxy.

Hexagenia nymphs are slightly darker on their dorsal than their ventral side, so as a finishing touch I use a tan or golden waterproof marking pen to color the top of the extended body. If you are so inclined, you can also touch up the top of the dubbing fibers that form the thorax. Try not to let the tail or gills come in contact with the colored areas until they dry: The moisture from the ink will often cause them to mat and they'll perform less well in the water.

The Rag Hex has been a wonderfully effective fly for me, but it's one pattern where the process of innovation may have been more valuable than the finished product. There are thousands of fly-tying materials out there, natural and synthetic, and new ones popping up daily. Some are of limited use but most possess potential. If you're an adventurous tier, you owe it to yourself to investigate as many materials as possible. Don't fall into the trap of assessing them based only on manufacturer suggestions—in many cases, an intrepid tier can invent novel uses for them that far surpass the ideas of the inventor, either by altering the material or simply thinking. And don't just look at it in the package: Buy a little, take it home, and get it wet. Even if you can't find an immediate use for the material, remember its properties. Somewhere down the line you're going to find the perfect application.

For me, such was the case with EZE Bug. Upon seeing and touching it for the first time, I dismissed it. I forced myself to tinker with it and eventually realized its potential as one of the more exciting large-fly synthetics on the market today.

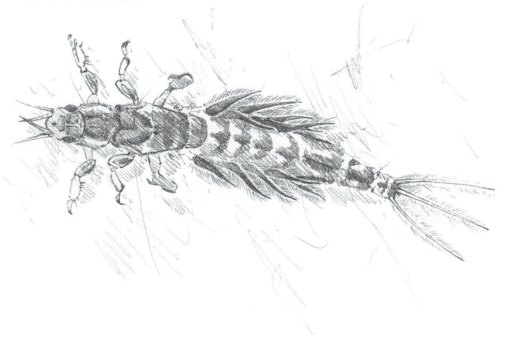

CHAPTER 11

ZEBRA MIDGELING

THE SNAKING TWO-LANE ROAD CLIMBED STEEPLY from the scorching valley floor, dropping heat like ballast as it climbed in elevation. As oaks gave way to manzanita outside, I notched back my air conditioning inside. The appearance of hardwoods motivated a deflection of the vents. Finally, with pine trees dominating the landscape blurring past, I opened my window and inhaled the cool, fresh mountain air. *Ah, life is good!*

I pulled off onto a short spur road, anticipation thudding in my chest as the lake came into view, its surface calm and unruffled. *Perfect.* Even better, I could see only one other angler, which guaranteed me a solitary experience. Parking, I quickly shouldered my float-tube and fins and gingerly tiptoed to the water's edge, praying that none of the stabbing pains I felt through my neoprene stocking feet would manifest themselves as hemorrhaging leaks. Successfully negotiating entry into the tube with fins attached, I sculled out a distance and, for the first time, took a close look at the water. I was surrounded not just by breathtaking scenery, but by dozens of trophy trout as well, their waggling dorsals betraying a mammoth emergence in progress. Everywhere I looked, there were fish! *Oh, no*, I despaired. *Not this again.*

ZEBRA MIDGELING

RECIPE

HOOK: TMC 2457 or 2487, depending on hook size

THREAD: Brown 8/0 UNI or to match fly color

TAIL: Pearl Angel Hair

RIB: Silver tying wire or to choice

UNDERBODY: Pearl Krystal Flash

BODY: Brown Midge Tubing or a color to match desired fly color

WING CASE: Pearl Krystal Flash

COLLAR: Brown ostrich herl or a color to match desired fly color

BEAD: Silver metal bead or color to choice, depending on fly color

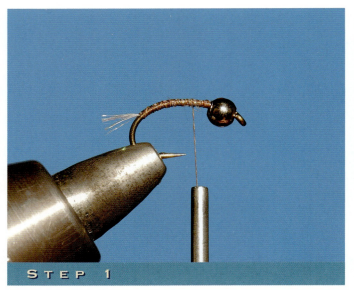

STEP 1

Slide a small bead (color to suit overall color scheme of fly) on the hook all the way to the eye. Form a sparse base with your thread from the bead back to a point just past the hook bend. Tie in a very sparse clump of pearl Angel Hair, wrapping it down from behind the bead, back past the bend of the hook. It should have a downward cant.

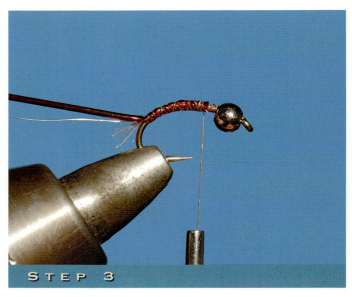

STEP 3

Tie in the body tubing—note the small space behind the bead that is left relatively open. This is important, as it helps when you are finishing the fly.

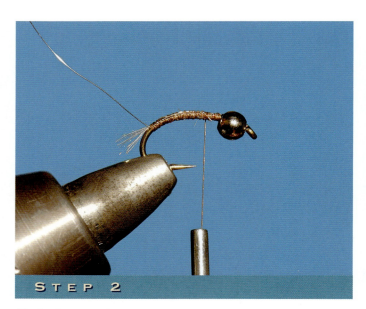

STEP 2

Tie in the wire rib, wrapping it down the length of the hook shank. On small flies such as this pattern, tying in everything at the same place eliminates undesirable bumps in body profiles.

STEP 4

Wrap in three strands of pearl Krystal Flash, following the same tie-down dimensions as the rib and body tubing. At this point you should have a thin, smooth underbody.

STEP 5

Wind the Krystal Flash forward evenly, tying off and clipping just behind bead.

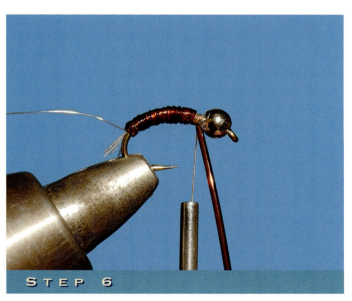

STEP 6

Repeat the above process with the body tubing. Stretch the tubing tightly while wrapping, ensuring a thin body. You'll find the tubing overlaps itself easily as you wind it forward.

This scene played out nearly two decades ago, at a time when I fished a lot and was becoming fairly accomplished with a fly rod. Much to my dismay, however, I had an Achilles heel, a dirty little secret that continually stymied me and eroded my confidence. In a word, midges. Specifically, the situation in still waters where trout keyed in on chironomid pupae as they hung in the water's surface film or wriggled just inches below. Characterized by the telltale dorsal or tail rise, and the visible absence of a fish's mouth, this scenario often spelled frustration for me. I was able to hook some fish, but my success rate was erratic. The fact that I would land a few trout one day, then virtually none the next, mystified me. What was I missing? Was it technique or pattern selection? How was it that I could fool the toughest spring-creek trout on the planet, then get worked by a bunch of ordinary lake fish every time their attention turned to minute insects? My answer? Fish more Woolly Buggers!

My first offshoot from the ubiquitous, original Zebra Midge.

What was I missing? How was it that I could fool the toughest spring-creek trout on the planet, then get worked by a bunch of ordinary lake fish every time their attention turned to minute insects?

Some time later, I had an epiphany while sharing a small reservoir in Oregon with a stranger. We were both fishing from prams. Through sheer tenacity, I was having a decent day, throwing (what else?) small olive Woolly Buggers to submerged weedbeds, continually moving and pounding this structure with the fervor and single-mindedness of a bass pro with a spinnerbait. While taking a break and enjoying a bite of lunch, I watched the other angler as he anchored up about 50 yards distant (with an anchor out each end of the boat, I observed—a bit of genius that kept his pram from swinging in the breeze and disrupting his presentations).

I noticed he spent a lot of time tinkering with his tackle. It was also impossible to ignore that he was catching

STEP 7

Wrap the wire rib forward, forming evenly spaced segmentation.

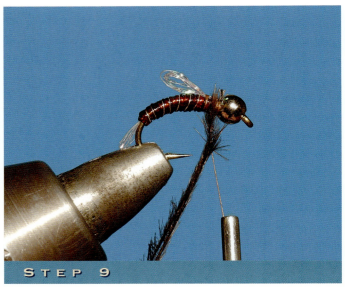

STEP 9

Tie in two ostrich herls by their tips, in front of the body. Twist the herls around the tying thread three to four times, to improve the ostrich's durability.

STEP 8

Tie in three to four strands of pearl Krystal Flash behind the bead, then bend it over on itself, forming a "loop" wing case that is approximately one-half the body length. Clip off excess.

STEP 10

Holding both the thread and the twisted herls, wrap a "head" out of the ostrich, effectively hiding all the tie-downs behind the bead. Clip excess herls and whip-finish. Leaving a gap between the material tie-downs and the bead facilitates the nearly invisible thread finish.

STEP 11

The finished Zebra Midgeling.

a lot of trout! As I watched, he caught three fish in quick succession, then nothing for about 10 minutes. A bit of tinkering. Four more fish, on the same number of casts, then a slow spell. More tinkering. Another three trout. And so it went until I couldn't stand it any more, and began to hammer away again with my streamers, catching the odd fish here and there.

As it happened, we were staying at the same lodge that night. Recognizing the guy, I approached him with congratulations on his fine day. Modestly deflecting the praise, he allowed as how it had been a rather productive day, though he'd had to really work for his fish.

A small Blood Midge variation I've found particularly effective in fishing tailwaters, or beneath an indicator in lakes.

As I watched, he caught three fish in quick succession, then nothing for about 10 minutes. A bit of tinkering. Four more fish, on the same number of casts, then a slow spell. More tinkering. Another three trout.

"Work?" I exclaimed. "Every time I turned around you were tight to another fish. I'd hate to see you on a really good day!" It turned out my fellow angler was Brian Chan, author and stillwater expert extraordinnaire. As I queried him about his success, he went into great detail concerning water depth, clarity, temperature, thermoclines, oxygenation and algal blooms (much of which was lost on me, of Woolly-Bugger mentality), but one observation stuck with me. As Brian and I discussed patterns, he mentioned that he had used almost nothing but midge pupae for the entire day. Surprised, as I'd seen none of the classic surface activity that would indicate emerging midges, I asked what made him try them.

"Well, I started with a Woolly Bugger, but when I realized that wasn't the ticket"—*Ouch!*—"I put on a long leader and a mayfly nymph. Again, not much happened, so I simply replaced the mayfly with a midge pupa, and that seemed to do the trick."

When I asked what all the tinkering had been about, Brian gave an answer involving details a nuclear physicist would have appreciated, but the gist of it was that he continually changed pupal pattern colors and the length of his tippet, searching for the trout's ever-changing dietary and geographical preferences. He then graciously offered a few of his flies, which I inspected closely later that evening. Unspectacular in appearance, they nonetheless all had a few characteristics in common; a slim profile, defined ribbing, and a bit of fluff emulating gills. One had a slightly translucent body, apparently due to the use of a colored material wrapped the length of the hook. I'd seen how they produced, and I anxiously awaited my chance to give them a spin.

As luck would have it, I didn't fish another lake for more than a year. When I did, it was a high-mountain pond known for its oversized and very selective rainbows. Autumn had arrived. With cool daytime temperatures came a distinct lack of insect activity. By mid-afternoon, having dredged up only a few fish by trolling dragonfly nymphs, I reluctantly conceded there would be no *Callibaetis* hatch and began working back toward shore. I stopped rowing when I caught the barest glimpse of a fish surfacing 50 feet away. As I watched, two more quietly breached, showing only back and a bit of dorsal. *Uh-oh*, I cringed, *those looked like midge grabs*.

Then all was quiet for a while. Mentally breathing a sigh of relief at being spared another humiliation, I started to put down my rod when I remembered Brian's bugs. Opening my box, I found them, still tucked away in a corner. I recalled his advice that if only a few fish are working surface emergers, there often will be many more intercepting the

was with interest that I considered the possibilities of fishing tiny midge patterns in some of my favorite rivers. No longer intimidated by the prospect of chironomids—neither their tiny dimensions nor the selectivity of trout when feeding on them—I decided to take them to a local waterway, the McCloud River.

For years I'd fished this classic freestoner in the spring and fall, and I loved the near-constant action from its famous inhabitants. The summer months, however, were a different story. The stoneflies of early runoff were over, sequestered back in their rocky haunts, and my favorite mayfly emergences were a memory, wilting in the season's heat. Caddisflies, which thrived in the scorching temperatures, were largely unavailable during daylight hours, leaving a gaping hole in the fishing day. I had always suspected trout continued to feed on the river's abundant midge populations during the midday heat, and I was soon to find out just how true this was.

Is this a midge or a micro-caddis? Who cares—trout love it!

I stopped rowing when I caught the barest glimpse of a fish surfacing 50 feet away. As I watched, two more quietly breached, showing only back and a bit of dorsal. *Uh-oh*, I cringed, *those looked like midge grabs*.

diminutive pupae at greater depths. Following his instructions, I knotted on an extra five feet of 6X, attached my favorite of his patterns, and stretched out a cast. Watching closely as the nymph gradually pulled the leader underwater, I began a painfully slow retrieve as the tippet knot disappeared. Halfway home, my leader twitched, I lifted tight to a huge rainbow, and my curse was ended. Since that day I've enjoyed countless memorable outings fishing chironomids in stillwater environs. I still get embarrassed sometimes, but that is as it should be—more important, I no longer wear the monkey of ignorance on my back. Now I approach these situations with a confidence necessary for success.

As with most fly fishers, the great bulk of my time on the water is spent on streams. The truth is, as much as I delight in plying lakes, I still prefer moving water. So it

I'd never forgotten my attraction to one of Brian's flies, the model tied with a translucent body. Having studied midge larvae and pupae sampled from waters close to home, I realized his feature was genius; combining it with some alterations of my own design resulted in the creation of the original Midgeling.

I came armed with this pattern one sweltering summer afternoon, deep within the leafy confines of The Nature Conservancy's McCloud Reserve. I'd hung the tiny bug a foot beneath a tungsten-beaded mayfly nymph, and crimped on a pair of BBs as well, to pull the flies tight on their eight-foot leash beneath a floating yarn indicator. I reasoned the trout wouldn't move far in the oppressive heat to take much of anything, much less a piddling little morsel like a midge. The flies would have to be right in their hunkered-down faces.

The word "silly" comes to mind when attempting to describe that day's success. I have no idea how many fish I hooked, but I eventually got past the giddy stage, and actually began to feel a little guilty. I think I know how the inventor of Powerbait must have felt the first time he lobbed a ball of the gunk into a tank of fish. Every good run yielded not just a fish or two, which would have elated me, but an embarrassment of hook-ups. To this day, it is one of the single greatest reactions to a new pattern that I've ever experienced.

that persuaded me to come up with a new incarnation.

First, the original Midgeling is tied with a glass bead head. A wonderful and realistic feature that selective trout seem to love, it nevertheless leaves the angler reliant on adding outside weight to get the fly down. For my new model, I replaced the glass bead with metal. Second, the overwhelming popularity of the simple Zebra Midge convinced me I was missing the boat by not incorporating a pronounced segmentation into my pattern. Additional research again proved the beauty of Brian

I eventually got past the giddy stage, and actually began to feel a little guilty. I think I know how the inventor of Powerbait must have felt the first time he lobbed a ball of the gunk into a tank of fish.

I'm sure I was about the millionth angler to discover this midge-pupa phenomenon, but at the time it was pure magic and a wonderful confirmation of the importance of the little critters in a trout's diet. No surprise, really, when you consider just how widespread and abundant they are in rivers everywhere.

For the next year I fished the Midgeling non-stop: during the heat of the day, the cool of evening, in the middle of a caddis hatch—it just didn't seem to matter. As good as it usually performed, though, two issues surfaced

Chan's original designs, as his pronounced ribbings closely emulated the naturals' body profiles. I added a colored wire rib, and the Zebra Midgeling was born.

In hindsight now, a few years later, I realize each style has its own application, and neither version really supplants the other. I still like the original for fishing as a dropper nymph in situations where a deep drift is necessary—this is especially true in tailwater fisheries. When the water is shallower, or the trout more aggressive, it's a blast to suspend a Zebra Midgeling beneath a favorite attractor dry. The metal bead head pulls the fly deep quickly, negating the need to add weight. This technique is especially popular in the Rockies, where I have found many fish, weary of seeing too many Pheasant Tails and Prince Nymphs, all too happy to suck down the Zebra. Also, when fishing lakes, both the *blip* of the beaded version entering the water and its quick sink-rate make it attractive to deeply cruising trout.

When choosing a hook for the Zebra Midgeling, I needed:

1. A chassis that would allow me to create a curved profile by tying beyond the hook bend.

2. Adequate gape to allow for good hooking capabilities even with a metal bead partially obscuring said gape.

3. A hook strong enough in even the smallest sizes to withstand the punishment of large trout on moderately heavy tippets.

This was an easy choice—TMC's 2457 was seemingly custom-designed for the purpose, and is available in sizes down to 18. For size 20 and smaller I use the TMC 2487; though lighter-wired than the 2457, it's quite func-

To emulate the naturals' pronounced abdominal segmentation, I utilize a wire rib. Since the real insects' intersegmental banding is often a lighter shade of their body color, I like to use a wire that recreates this effect. For example, on an olive pupa, I'll use a bright green rib; on a brown model, copper wire. On black, one of the pattern's most popular colors, I like a silver rib, just as on the more traditional Zebra Midge. Finally, if the fly is of a light or medium hue, I'll often run a dark brown waterproof marking pen down the entire dorsal length of the abdomen—this mirrors a common natural coloration of many midge pupae.

If I were forced to omit one step in the construction of this fly, the wing case would be the last to go. Though the fly has many potential triggers built in, I believe this single feature may be the most important. As an experiment, I once tied one onto a hook that was bare, save for a single layer of thread covering the shank. I caught fish. I followed by using just the thread-covered hook, sans the wing case. Nothing. When I added a wire rib, I caught a couple, but not nearly as many as with the wing case.

> **When the water is shallower, or the trout more aggressive, it's a blast to suspend a Zebra Midgeling beneath a favorite attractor dry. The metal bead head pulls the fly deep quickly, negating the need to add weight.**

tional with the light tippets employed with a fly this size.

Actual chironomid pupae breathe through two sets of gills, one at their head and another in the tail region. While many patterns employ white materials of various types to imitate the abdominal tufts, I was more concerned with the flash given off by the air trapped in those gills. With this in mind, I used a very short, sparse clump of pearl Angel Hair for a tail. Be aware that a little of this material goes a long way—remember that you're imitating just a glint of refracted light. Too much flash will spook fish, not attract them.

Look closely at many emerging midge pupae, and you'll notice they are translucent, to varying degrees. They also employ a layer of trapped air beneath their pupal skin to aid in their ascent from the stream bottom; as with the gills, this air gives off a reflective sheen, a feature I have to believe trout key in on. To mimic this effect, I created an underbody of wrapped Krystal Flash, covered by an overbody of tightly wound transparent tubing. I choose the tubing color to match the insect in question; the color of Krystal Flash doesn't seem to make much difference, as it is largely diffused by the tubing color. When tying this abdomen, remember that actual midge pupae have extremely slender bodies. To avoid unnecessary and unwanted bulk, use only a few strands of Krystal Flash for the underbody. The smallest possible tubing should also be used, and stretched as much as possible when wrapping it forward, to achieve its smallest diameter.

Since then, I've substituted this style on many other patterns, with great success. It's easy to construct: Simply tie in three to four strands of pearl Krystal Flash so the ends lay back over the body, then pull them forward so they form a small, tight loop over the front of the abdomen. That's it!

I wish I could claim the idea was mine, but it'd be a lie—it came to me via a singularly unattractive little fly given to me by a friend, along with the claim that it just murdered trout everywhere he used it. I took a quick look, memorized the wing-case design, and when he wasn't watching I tossed the repulsive little thing. Incidentally, it's not lost on me that the actual insects' wing pads are located on the sides of the body and not the top. But tying in two separate loops is a pain in the neck and has proven absolutely no more effective—perhaps less so my guess is this feature suggests the splitting husk of the emerging insect, as much as actual wing pads.

Up to this point, the fly looks very lifelike but sports virtually no material motion to suggest life—this goes against one of my most fundamental rules of fly design, particularly for nymphs. To remedy, I tie in one or two ostrich herls (the color of which I select to complement the abdomen coloration), wrap them around the tying thread to reinforce against being cut by sharp teeth, then wind on to imitate legs or gills. Works like a charm.

Of course, the pattern would be incomplete without a metal bead head. Though I like a silver bead on the

**As fly fishers and tiers, we all owe
a significant percentage of our success to
the innovations of others—certainly the
evolution of the Zebra Midgeling
is an example of that truth**

black fly, and copper on most others, I think you should experiment here, to see what works best for you. An effective option is to use a tungsten bead; even the tiniest pupa will plummet through the water column with one of these strapped to its cranium.

As fly fishers and tiers, we all owe a significant percentage of our success to the innovations of others—certainly the evolution of the Zebra Midgeling is an example of that truth. I'll never be as adept a stillwater angler as Brian Chan, but thanks to his generous spirit and well-designed patterns, I now approach lake fishing and tying with an enthusiasm I might not otherwise have achieved.

To the mystery tier who gave me the idea for the Midgeling's wing case, a tip of my hat. And to whatever minimalist genius that came up with the original Zebra Midge—I'm eternally jealous.

GLASSTAIL CADDIS PUPA

HAVE YOU EVER STOPPED TO CONSIDER the process of emergence in aquatic insects? I mean, have you really thought about the concept?

What an incredible transformation it is, beginning with thousands of complex, gilled, underwater-dwelling little insects, all perfectly adapted to their environment through eons of evolution. They spend their lives, presumably, without the slightest inkling that big changes are in the future, blissfully oblivious to the inevitable metamorphosis occurring within their skins. Suddenly, at a cosmically pre-appointed moment—often nearly in unison—all the bugs are drawn upwards, like marionettes on invisible strings.

Do they know what's going on? They struggle, but is it to complete their fate, or fight against the strange new buoyancy? Without warning, they reach the glass ceiling, finding themselves like so many diminutive overturned turtles, legs struggling, but going nowhere. Wondering, no doubt, what's next?

GLASSTAIL CADDIS PUPA

RECIPE

HOOK: TMC 2457, size 12-16

TYING THREAD: 8/0 UNI or equivalent to match fly color

THREAD USED FOR EXTENDED BODY CORE: Smallest available diameter Kevlar thread

EXTENDED BODY BEADS: Glass, color to match the real insect, tapered sizes if desired

BODY BEADS ON HOOK: Same as above

HEAD BEAD ON HOOK: Gunmetal or peacock-color glass bead

BODY DUBBING: Mercer's Select Buggy Nymph, Amber Caddis, or to match bead color used

ANTENNAE: Lemon-barred wood-duck flank fibers

LEGS: Golden-brown mottled hen back or grouse feather

WING CASE: Brown Thin Skin

COLLAR: Peacock herl

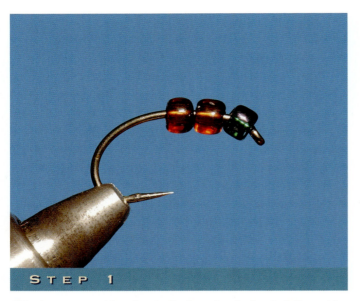

STEP 1

Slip the gunmetal bead onto the bare hook shank, followed by two of the amber.

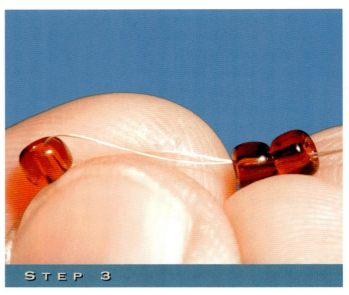

STEP 3

Loop one end of the thread around an end bead, then feed it back through the other two beads. The abdomen is finished.

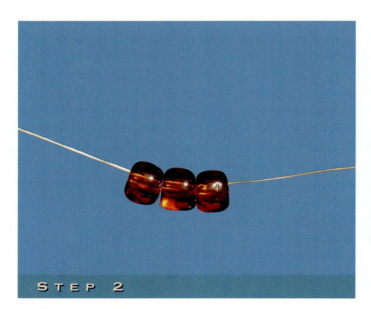

STEP 2

Begin forming the extended abdomen by threading three amber beads onto a length of Kevlar thread. (An interesting option is to use progressively smaller-sized beads in this trio, creating the illusion of a tapered abdomen.)

STEP 4

Attach tying thread to the hook shank behind the beads, forming a thin thread base. Lay both ends of the doubled thread from the extended body on top of the hook shank, pointing forward. Wrap them down with tying thread from the rear of the hook to a point just behind the glass beads on the hook shank. Now tug the two ends of Kevlar tightly enough so that the bead abdomen holds in place, but not so tightly as to prevent any movement from them.

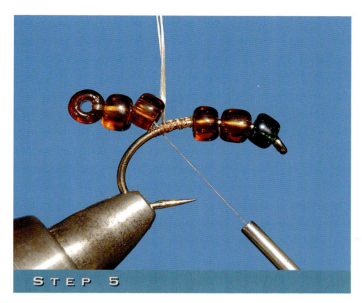

STEP 5

Pull the doubled threads back over the hook shank, so they point rearward, and wrap back over them with the tying thread. Repeat the above steps, pulling the threads forward again, wrapping them down, and finish by bringing them back and tying them down a final time. These steps are critical to securing the abdomen to the hook; the Kevlar thread is slippery, and anything less will allow the extended body to slip off while fishing.

STEP 6

Form a dubbing loop just in front of the abdomen.

The fun has just begun. In the blink of an eye, the skin on their back splits open, and *presto*, out come . . . WINGS! Just like that, a creature that has spent all of its life swimming and crawling is airborne, using strange new appendages to soar high above all it has ever known.

Imagine waking up one morning, 50 years old, stuck to the bedroom ceiling by your back. Before you can even scream for help, the roof of your house dissolves, you discover enormous five-foot wings sprouted from your shoulders, and you're up! Quite possibly insects don't experience the same sort of wonder we humans do; but personally, I hope they do. No matter how many times I watch this quiet drama unfold, I never lose my sense of awe, my feelings of amazement regarding yet another of Nature's magic cycles.

Emerald beads create a striking pupa: A color variation effective from coast to coast, particularly during spring emegences.

> ### Somewhere far off, a mourning dove murmured its sad call. Then, directly in front of me, a fish rose, and all else fell from focus.

It was late March. The lower Sacramento was running wide and clear. Spring was in the air. I knelt briefly at the water's edge, breathing the loamy musk of the riverbottom, drinking in the cool, fresh aroma of the sliding currents. A profusion of bankside wildflowers nodded sleepily in the warm evening breeze, their bright hues fading with the setting sun. Somewhere far off, a mourning dove murmured its sad call. Then, directly in front of me, a fish rose, and all else fell from focus. Watching the drifting rings, I thought about the riseform. No part of the trout had shown itself—there was only a quick push of water, dissolving into oily turbulence. Emerger grab.

I had no doubt regarding what the fish had eaten. The Mother's Day Caddis emergence, *Brachycentrus occidentalis*, was in full swing, with trout levitating to the surface nightly, greedily intercepting as many of the little squiggling morsels as possible. So it was with utmost

STEP 7

Insert a dubbing twister into the bottom of the loop, and clumps of dubbing throughout its length.

STEP 9

Make a single revolution of the dubbing brush against the extended body. Push the rearmost of the hook shank beads back tightly against the dubbing.

STEP 8

Use the twister to form a dubbing "brush."

STEP 10

Jump the dubbing brush over this bead (try and make the jump on the underside of the body), and make a single revolution around the shank with it.

Repeat the previous step, then tie off the dubbing brush and trim the excess. I like to take a dubbing teaser at this point, and comb the dubbing to the bottom and sides of the beads. This effectively covers the bottom portion of the fly, while leaving the tops of the beads showing above the dubbing. When the fly gets wet, this configuration gives a realistic and striking visual effect.

Select two evenly matched lemon barred wood duck flank feathers, and tie them over the top of the body of the fly—they should reach approximately as far back as the end of the extended body.

confidence that I knotted on a small green nymph four feet beneath a tuft of buoyant yarn, laid a cast well upstream of where I'd seen the take, and fed line into the dead-drift. Sure enough, midway through the float the bright bobber popped beneath the surface, and I came tight to an extraordinarily annoyed rainbow.

A great start to a great evening, I thought to myself, hurrying to land the fish and go for another.

An hour later, enveloped in the cloak of dusk and with not another fish to my fly, I found myself wishing I'd reveled in the satisfaction of that first trout a bit more. As I anticipated, the river had come alive with gorging fish; unexpectedly, my Midas touch had turned to coal. It was bizarre, really—fish feeding everywhere, and I knew on what, but I was helpless to hook even one. Bewildered, I headed home, vowing to return the next night, with a plan.

View from above highlights the bead "segmentation," dark, iridescent head, and messy, realistic appendages.

No part of the trout had shown itself— there was only a quick push of water, dissolving into oily turbulence. Emerger grab.

I thought about the humbling all the next day, trying hard to understand why the fish had turned completely off my fly. It was a proven pattern, a sort of beadhead soft hackle tied by one of my guide friends, which in the past had accounted for plenty of trout keying on the river's emerging caddisflies.

Perhaps it wasn't the fly at all, I considered—maybe it was my presentation. After all, the trout were used to seeing thousands of emergers struggling to the surface. Maybe I needed to take off the indicator and swing the fly, using short strips to emulate the thrashing pupae. Full of confidence once more, and excited by the prospect of trying something new, I left work with a new leader at the end of my floating line, rigged with a brace of small olive caddisfly wets.

STEP 13

Select a golden-brown mottled henback or grouse breast feather, stripping all of the fluff off the bottom of the stem. Tie the bare stem onto the hook shank immediately in front of the body.

STEP 15

As you wrap back over these hackles to force them into a "backswept" position, manipulate the fibers with your fingers so they enfold most of the body, but are absent over the very top of the fly. If you have difficulty with this technique, no problem—simply trim the fibers that extend over the top of the fly.

STEP 14

Take two wraps of the soft hackle around the hook shank, then tie it off and clip the excess feather. You'll know that you selected the right size hackle if, when pushed backwards with your finger, the tips extend to about the bend of the hook.

STEP 16

Cut a narrow strip of Thin Skin, and tie one end down on top of the hook shank. Wrap back over it with your thread until it butts up firmly against the body of the fly.

STEP 17

Tie in two to three strands of peacock herl by the tips, then take three to four wraps of them around the tying thread (this will essentially make a peacock "brush", greatly improving the durability of the material in the finished fly).

STEP 18

Wrap the peacock brush forward two to four times, to the point where it butts up against the forward bead. Tie off the peacock and clip the excess.

As I pulled off the road and parked beneath a familiar spreading oak, inhaling the last bite of what passed for a cheeseburger, I noted with satisfaction that no other vehicles were present—I'd likely have the run all to myself again. Taking a last, longing gaze at my uneaten french fries (fishing schedules sometimes exact a terrible toll on my dining habits), I pulled on waders and shoes, strapped on my fanny pack, grabbed my rod and set off at a brisk pace through the brush. Arriving at the river, I was greeted not only by a dearth of other anglers, as expected, but also by a shallow flat alive with boiling trout.

The grab was already on!

Casting across and down, I kept my rod tip close to the water, using my line hand to twitch the flies seductively through areas of working fish.

Just hang on, I told myself, *don't snap 'em off on the strike*. Fifty presentations later, that seemed the least of my worries—I had to get a grab before I could be concerned with breaking it off.

> **The fat, wriggling caddisfly pupa, freshly plucked from the trout's jaw, tried desperately to convulse free of my fingers. As I held it up to the fading sun, I marveled at the beauty of the tiny creature, in particular its translucent banding. *It's like looking through glass*, I recall thinking.**

So, I did what I always do when faced with this situation: I tried every fly in my box.

To be fair, this is not always such a misguided ploy as one might suppose; in fact, it has consistently rewarded me with mediocre results. And trust me, when faced with humiliating defeat, a good old-fashioned dose of mediocrity starts looking pretty attractive. Along about the fifth pattern, my indicator dipped (yep, I lost confidence in the swinging deal) and I was fast to a fish.

Landing the trout, I took a moment to admire it. Typical for the lower Sac, it was vividly marked, heavy-shouldered and deep of belly, 18 inches of perfection on fins. Then, just as I prepared to slide it back, a flash of brilliant color caught my eye, from near the fish's head. Looking closer, I discovered the trout's mouth was a veritable minefield of luminescence, explosive bits of squirming caddisfly biomass trapped in the jaws, gills, on the tongue—everywhere. Obviously, this fish had paid extra to get the "all-you-can-eat" menu. Pulling a sample from his lips, I watched the rainbow drift back in the direction of his buffet line.

The fat, wriggling caddisfly pupa, freshly plucked from the trout's jaw, tried desperately to convulse free of

Pull the Thin Skin over the top of the peacock, forming a wing case. Tie the material off right against the front bead, trimming off all the excess. Whip finish and trim the thread.

The finished Glasstail Caddis Pupa.

my fingers. As I held it up to the fading sun, I marveled at the beauty of the tiny creature, in particular its translucent banding. *It's like looking through glass*, I recall thinking. I wondered how long it had been since this little guy was contentedly crawling around the streambed, happily gobbling microscopic pabulum, not a care in the world. I wondered what had prompted him to decide it was time to close up shop, lock the door to his modest home and drift off to sleep.

I imagined what it must have been like for him to jerk suddenly awake and find himself in a new body, a physique no longer encumbered by a portable prison, and even more amazing, able to swim for the first time in his life. No more creeping along the bottom like a bug—he could *swim!* (Still like a bug, granted, but hey, it's got to beat creeping.)

Then, just as he was getting the hang of that—BAM!—his skin unzips (this time while he's awake—*yikes*) and he's on Mars. Check that, he's flying above Mars, with his newfound giant wings!

Well, thanks to a hungry wild trout, this guy had missed out on that last big surprise, but I was determined to let him help me exact a certain vengeance back on the finned offenders. Examining the insect, I forced myself to note my first impressions, the "broad brushstrokes" for a fly designer: smallish (probably size 16), plump, light green abdomen tapered only moderately towards the tail, nearly translucent, dark head area.

Next, I looked more closely, hoping to glean some hidden detail which, if imitated in a fly, could prove to be that elusive triggering mechanism all tiers strive for.

I noticed the abdominal segments on the dorsal side of the pupa were distinctly darker than the belly. The head was actually iridescent, kind of a purplish black. Also, the legs were long, sort of messy and almost completely on the underside of the body. The antennae were body-length and appeared mottled. Interestingly, the wings, while apparent, blended with the body, appearing only as a vague darkening on the sides of the bug, extending to a point completely beneath the abdomen.

I wasn't able to tie for the next few days, which turned out to be a good thing. I couldn't stop thinking about the little pupa, and took endless trips each day from my desk to the tying materials section of the fly shop where I work, tinkering. It took a while, but a series of bits and pieces finally coalesced in my mind, into what would become the first version of the Glasstail Caddis Pupa.

For a couple of years, I'd admired the Pulsating Caddis pattern from the vise of local guide Jim Pettis. He was one of the first tiers I'd seen incorporate glass beads into the body of a caddis pupa. The result was magical. In the vise, the fly was nothing special, appearing much like 100 other basic caddisfly patterns. Add water, however, and the beads became visible, adding both segmentation and translucence to the effect. The fly was deadly. So it was that as I was trying to solve the riddle of transparence, the Pulsator came to mind.

Something about Jim's pattern had always bothered me, though, and I realized now it was the fly's silhouette—obviously good enough for the trout, but just too abbreviated to my eye. I came up with the idea of an extended body created with beads strung together, which also possessed the inherent potential of creating a taper by varying bead sizes. Eventually, this notion provided the basic framework for an entire series of patterns, but, in the short run, I still had to bring the visualized concept to fruition.

First I slid the requisite number of beads onto a single core to assure the proper length, graduated in size from largest to smallest. Taking the end of the core protruding from the smallest bead, I folded it over that bead and fed it back through the hole of the bead adjacent to it, and then sequentially through the holes of the rest of the beads. When the core emerged from the last bead, I had my extended body.

At this point, the question became: What to use for a core to string the beads onto? My first attempt was with monofilament. It seemed like a good idea, but in practical use its flaws quickly became apparent. First, if I used line

One of the beauties of the Glasstail design is that it frees me from the constraints of a particular hook format. I can create any style of extended body, any size or color, tapered or not, then simply attach it to a hook.

My first challenge was physically creating an extended bead body. Stringing the beads onto a core was obvious, but how to keep them from sliding off was not. After many failed and unsatisfactory results, I hit upon a surprisingly simple method that worked. I would determine how long I wanted the extended body to be, and how much, if any taper I desired.

heavier than eight-pound test, it proved far too stiff, and didn't allow for any movement of the bead abdomen. When I dropped down to mono light enough to let the beads move more freely, the first fish that ate the bug often broke it, ripping the body right off the hook. Strike one.

Next I tried thread, starting with size A Monocord, realizing that anything less would meet the same fate as small mono. Surprisingly, even this proved too stiff, and still not strong enough—the worst of both worlds. Strike two.

Finally, I hit on the idea of trying Kevlar thread. Though this product comes in several diameters, I was fortunate to randomly pick a small version the first time out of the gate. It worked. Tiny in diameter, it fit through even the smallest Czech glass beads, was limp enough to allow abdominal movement, and proved extremely strong.

There were only two challenges, both relatively easy to overcome. One, I needed a very sharp pair of scissors to smoothly trim the thread; anything less would just fray the multi-fibered product, making it impossible to work with. Two, the thread was extremely slippery. Simply tying the loose ends protruding from the extended glass body to the hook was inadequate—the first fish would pull the abdomen right off the shank. So, when tying the thread ends to the hook shank, I first wrapped them down so the body was snug against the hook, then folded the ends

To complete the effect, I borrowed an idea from Jim Pettis, and dubbed much of the thorax. Starting at the point where the extended body was tied on, I dubbed a single wrap, then jumped forward over the next bead and took another single wind of dubbed thread. Continuing forward in this manner, I finished with a dubbing wrap in between each thorax bead, and in front of the most forward thoracic bead. I then used a dubbing teaser to draw the bulk of the dubbing towards the bottom of the pattern (to hide the dark bottom half of the beads), and trimmed the remaining dubbing flush with the beads on the top 100-degrees or so of the fly. When immersed, this combination provided a wonderfully realistic effect.

I decided that to keep the pattern somewhat anatomically correct, I would tie in legs and antennae. I settled on hen back fiber legs, as they're easy and cheap to acquire, are soft and undulate in the water, and the legs of my actual model had been similarly dark and opaque. (An attractive substitute would be grouse or brown partridge.) Attached as a 180-degree hackle, the fibers'

Satisfied with the profile and translucence of the fly thus far, my next goal was to emulate the darkened dorsal segments I'd noticed on the natural. To do this, of course, I had to create a belly that was a much lighter shade, to provide the contrast.

over so they faced toward the rear of the hook, and wrapped over them again. I then repeated this by folding them forward and wrapping over them a third time. At this point, the body tie-down was secure—it could not slip out from under the thread wraps.

One of the beauties of the Glasstail design is that it frees me from the constraints of a particular hook format. I can create any style of extended body, any size or color, tapered or not, then simply attach it to a hook. Compared to the inflexibility of having to slide beads onto a hook, and being forced to live within the creative boundaries that hook shape allows, I find this technique to be quite liberating. When considering which hook would best suit my purpose, I realized it would need to be a short-shank model. With the abdomen (typically the longest part of most insects' physique) already accounted for, a shorter hook would provide more than enough chassis to accommodate the thorax portion of the tie. Because I often hook large trout in heavy currents, I wanted a strong hook, as well. My choice was the TMC 2457.

Satisfied with the profile and translucence of the fly thus far, my next goal was to emulate the darkened dorsal segments I'd noticed on the natural. To do this, of course, I had to create a belly that was a much lighter shade, to provide the contrast. I already knew I was going to slide several beads onto the hook, to create a look of continuity with the abdomen (in addition to a single, iridescent bead for the head)—that these would provide realistic, darkened upper-body segments solved half my problem.

length was about equal to that of the hook shank. For the antennae, I tied in a pair of lemon wood duck-fibers, one on each side of the body, so they pointed backwards and up, stretching to about the same length as the extended body.

Examining the real caddisfly pupa some days earlier, I'd noticed that in addition to possessing an iridescent head, the very front of the insect also had notably darker body segments. The iridescence was easy to imitate—there may not be a single more effective tying material on the planet than peacock herl. A couple of herls twisted around the tying thread and then wrapped forward virtually guaranteed the fly a reasonable modicum of success, all by itself. Crowning the peacock, to replicate the top of this darker forward segment, I tied in a short "wing case" of brown Thin Skin. Tied off against the darkly opalescent "head" bead, it completed the effect.

Though the glass-bead revolution has never really gained much momentum, these little colored spheres have a lot to offer the intrepid tier. Translucence, myriad size and color choices, and a shape that closely resembles the individual body segments of many aquatic insects are but a few of their provocative attributes. I use them in many of my nymph, streamer and even dry-fly patterns, and have come to believe in their irresistible appeal to fish. They work.

SPECIAL OPPORTUNITY FOR COLLECTORS

For collectors interested in an authentic set of the original flies featured in **Creative Fly Tying**, Wild River Press has arranged with the author and Angler's Choice Framing—the foremost museum-quality framer of flies in America—to produce a limited-edition shadowbox presentation of all 12 patterns. Each trout fly is tied personally and with meticulous care by designer Mike Mercer. A limited edition copy of this book, signed and numbered by the author, accompanies each set of original flies. The book comes in an embossed, handmade lambskin slipcase. A special Mike Mercer Signature Selection of fishing flies in a beautiful custom-made hardwood fly box crafted in New Zealand is also available. For more information about this and other fine products related to the series **Masters on the Fly**, please visit www.wildriverpress.com or e-mail premium@wildriverpress.com.

WILD RIVER PRESS
Post Office Box 13360
Mill Creek, Washington 98082 USA

AFTERWORD

AS A FLY TIER, MY BIZARRE BRAIN SEES THE OUTSIDE WORLD through a different lens than most. Occasionally this is a good thing. Whenever this near-constant state of aberrational thought happens to spit out something of possible interest, even if totally out of context with what I'm working on at the moment, I write it down. It's a habit I've developed over the years. A quick scribble of an idea, a brief sketch to see how it might look—anything to ensure against the loss of the one precious idea!

Consequently, my tying desk resembles nothing so much as the streets of Times Square on New Year's morning, littered with the confetti of my imagination. At least once a year I sort through all these scraps, re-examining them in the cold light of reality (or at least as close as I'm likely to get). Fully half of these gems go immediately into the trash; one quarter go into the look-at-again-in-six-months file; the remaining quarter actually make it to the vise.

It's worth noting that many of my original ideas are tweaked considerably as I attempt to turn rough concepts into useful outcomes. In the end, some of my early visions of nymphs get transformed to emergers; emergers hatch to full-blown dries. You just never know. *You must keep an open mind.*

If you are serious about becoming an innovative fly tier, I strongly suggest you keep notes. Give them time to marinate. Don't ever try to force the creative process. If it's right, it will follow.

Remember, you may extract a single feature from one of my flies, and incorporate it in an innovative pattern of your own design. Nothing would make me happier. After all, most patterns in this book are compilations of individual ideas borrowed from others, strung together in a signature manner on a hook. You're probably more organized than I am. So go ahead and use the following pages to doodle, make notes and invent—exploring and documenting your own satisfying path of creative fly tying.

MM

INDEX